TEACHING ENGLISH and MATHS in FE

Sara Miller McCune founded SAGE Publishing in 1965 to support the dissemination of usable knowledge and educate a global community. SAGE publishes more than 1000 journals and over 800 new books each year, spanning a wide range of subject areas. Our growing selection of library products includes archives, data, case studies and video. SAGE remains majority owned by our founder and after her lifetime will become owned by a charitable trust that secures the company's continued independence.

Los Angeles | London | New Delhi | Singapore | Washington DC | Melbourne

TEACHING ENGLISH and MATHS in FE

WHAT WORKS FOR VOCATIONAL LEARNERS?

DAVID ALLAN

Learning Matters
An imprint of SAGE Publications Ltd
1 Oliver's Yard
55 City Road
London EC1Y 1SP

SAGE Publications Inc.
2455 Teller Road
Thousand Oaks, California 91320

SAGE Publications India Pvt Ltd
B 1/I 1 Mohan Cooperative Industrial Area
Mathura Road
New Delhi 110 044

SAGE Publications Asia-Pacific Pte Ltd
3 Church Street
#10-04 Samsung Hub
Singapore 049483

Editor: Amy Thornton
Development editor: Jennifer Clark
Production controller: Chris Marke
Project management: Swales and Willis Ltd, Exeter, Devon
Marketing manager: Dilhara Attygalle
Cover design: Wendy Scott
Typeset by: C&M Digitals (P) Ltd, Chennai, India
Printed and bound by CPI Group (UK) Ltd, Croydon, CR0 4YY

Library of Congress Number: 2017936976

British Library Cataloguing in Publication Data

A catalogue record for this book is available from the British Library

ISBN 978-1-4739-9278-8
ISBN 978-1-4739-9279-5 (pbk)

At SAGE we take sustainability seriously. Most of our products are printed in the UK using FSC papers and boards. When we print overseas we ensure sustainable papers are used as measured by the PREPS grading system. We undertake an annual audit to monitor our sustainability.

Contents

Acknowledgements

I would like to thank the following people who have been supportive in the process of initiating, and writing, this book:

My mum and dad, Margaret and Anthony, for their drive (and ability to eventually forgive me for walking out of an apprenticeship when I was younger). My brother Tony, for his advice and willingness to help without question. My wife Venetia, for always being 100 per cent behind me. My stepsons Daniel and Jamie for their enthusiasm and encouragement. My baby daughter Sophie, for being an inspiration.

Amy Thornton, the Senior Commissioning Editor (Education), for advice and support throughout. Jennifer Clark, the Development Editor, for her encouraging feedback and excellent guidance. Dr Vicky Duckworth for helping me get the project off the ground. The FET team and many others in the Faculty of Education at Edge Hill University who I unfortunately cannot name individually.

About the author

David Allan

David Allan is a lecturer in Further Education and Training at Edge Hill University and holds a PhD in educational research from Lancaster University. He is currently leading on a number of research projects within education which involve working with schools and colleges across the country. David has previously worked as a tutor in adult and community education and as a lecturer in the FE and skills sector, where he taught both English and maths as skills for life, as functional skills, and as GCSEs for over ten years.

In his current role, David has undertaken international, collaborative research with a number of higher education institutions in Georgia and Armenia. His latest project – the result of the securement of a large international bid to develop teaching methodologies in vocational areas – involves 12 universities in Vietnam, Laos, Romania, Ireland and Germany.

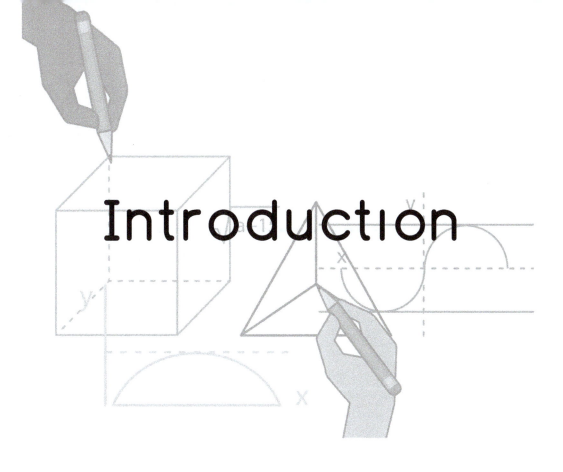

Introduction

We have set a new level of ambition for the sector for the attainment of maths and English for post-16 learners so that any young person without a good pass in GCSE at age 16 … should be supported to achieve this.

(DBIS, 2014, p4)

As can be seen from the above quote, the teaching and/or embedding of English and maths is now a major concern for the FE and skills sector, and institutions are rising to meet the demands of the new conditions of funding. Consequently, the professional development needs of many teachers is changing and some are uncomfortable with, and even anxious about, moving into teaching subjects they perhaps weren't trained for.

This book, then, is aimed at teachers at all levels in the sector. Whether you are a trainee teacher about to embark on your placement, or an experienced lecturer where English and maths have traditionally been regarded as separate subjects to your own, this book is for you. It is about strategies for teaching and embedding maths and English, but it is also about raising awareness and drawing on the multitude of skills, experiences, and vast knowledge that you and your students have already acquired throughout your lives.

Some FE teachers have worked in industry, and have taught a vocational area, for many years, but never strictly maths and English. In some instances, there is actual fear, but this need not be so. These experienced professionals are missing a wonderful trick. They do not see the skills they have – perhaps because they have been through a system that has undervalued them – and many may feel that they are being asked to suddenly 'down tools' to explore imagery in the works of Shakespeare, or to simplify complex algebraic expressions, and become prize-winning *Countdown* contestants overnight. While these options are certainly open to you, your primary role as an FE teacher is to deliver your subject, with maths and English merely complementing this process. Teaching maths and English can be both easy and fun, and this book will hopefully dispel some myths and illustrate a range of strategies and ideas that you can use and develop.

Reference

DBIS [Department for Business, Innovation and Skills] (2014) *Further Education Workforce Strategy*. London: Department for Business, Innovation and Skills.

1
Incorporating English and maths

 This chapter

This chapter explores the incorporation of maths and English in all teaching areas. It focuses on key features of embedding and the need to enthuse learners by drawing on personal goals to ensure learning is both relevant and inspirational. The chapter provides an overview of what is required to successfully embed English and maths for your learners.

This chapter supports you to:

- Get to know your students.
- Identify aspects of English and maths and emphasise what your students can do.
- Build on students' strengths and utilise their ambitions and personal interests.
- Support and praise.
- Build confidence and self-esteem.
- Be inclusive.
- Identify areas for improvement.
- Build on experience.

Get to know your students

Knowing your students is essential for good teaching and this knowledge is a key feature of planning. You may have a scheme of work in place, you may have detailed lesson plans to accompany every session, but you will still need to adapt these plans as you get to know who you are teaching (and why) and what their strengths and weaknesses are. Does a certain student scream and run out of the classroom when you mention fractions, for instance? Or break down in tears when they attempt them? These examples may sound extreme but they are taken from real-life events. You will therefore need to at least have a basic awareness of what is going on in your students' lives, and how this can impact on their learning. This does not mean prying into their personal life, of course; rather, it is about getting to know how you can help them to develop in the most efficacious manner. For instance, can you use their experiences to develop the embedding process? Consider the following example:

> *Ranjit regularly writes for a blog on his favourite subject: magic. He is a part-time magician and a member of his local magic circle.*

Can you use this information to bring a little magic to your lesson? (Pun intended.) The internet will be helpful here if you wish to seek out a magical number trick (or ask Ranjit to prepare one). You may find one that appears to draw on probability (but actually works every time), whereupon you can explore this further. Moreover, could Ranjit be asked to work collaboratively with other students? Would he mind writing about his experience of mixing magic with maths? This is likely to generate a lot more interest than merely looking at probability on its own.

Also, you will benefit greatly from understanding how your students function in the environment. Do the lights provide a glare for some students? Is the whiteboard unreadable for others? These are general teaching strategies and such pedagogical knowledge can be found in various books on teaching in FE. These, and many others, are worth exploring because they can play a major role in whether your students will learn or not. After all, if they have had poor experiences of English and maths at school, the addition of other barriers will only complicate matters.

 —— Learning exercise ——

For each of your students, list two pieces of information that you know about them but that is not related to the course. Can this information be useful for your planning?

Identify aspects of English and maths and emphasise what your students can do

This is particularly important for embedding English and maths because for a lot of your students, these areas will seem irrelevant and merely 'bolted on' to their course. You will need to illustrate that although English and maths are subjects in their own right, they are also essential ingredients of the subjects your students are studying. For instance, they may know to use twice as much peroxide as tint to colour hair but do they recognise that through this process they have begun to understand ratio?

Use personal experiences to tailor your teaching to personal needs and tastes in order to challenge individual weaknesses. For example, if you know a particular student has barriers with maths, you may wish to embed some of these skills within an activity (without making them explicit for the student), and point out what skills they have achieved once they are happy that they have met the session's aim. This can help to reduce poor perceptions of ability.

Build on students' strengths and utilise their ambitions and personal interests

You may have a student who would love to have completed an A level in English yet exhibits poor linguistic ability. What *can* she do? Does she excel in some areas yet (perhaps through barriers in perceived ability) struggle to achieve in others? In this instance, her ambition is a definite strength and it can be used to overcome her fears.

What are your students' interests and/or hobbies? This is contextual information that can be drawn on to maximise the efficiency of your teaching. Does Fred love fishing yet you regularly refer to this as a boring activity? Has Fred switched off through lack of respect or because you have failed to stimulate him? Does he have his own perception – now fuelled by your teaching – of what is boring? Perhaps Fred's contempt for reading is associated with school textbooks and mindless copying, or meaningless reading exercises. Did he merely skim over the words when asked to read at school? Has he reached his fifty-first birthday, despite the fact that his reading ability lies around Year 9? What fishing magazines are there to stimulate his interest in reading and to rebuild his confidence? Can you find an extract and use this for an activity? This may not be the subject that you are teaching but it could provide an essential bridge to steer Fred into other reading activities. Arguably, Fred does not link reading with fun and it is your job to build this connection.

Support and praise

Tasmin has demonstrated that she can calculate area as part of her tiling course. Before you move her on to the next activity, give her praise for this achievement. The phrase 'Well done!' often works wonders. Your students have worked hard to achieve and most will wish to impress you. Show them that they have. Are they familiar with the assessment criteria? Perhaps you can *tick off* this achievement in the breakdown. This will help them to understand how such achievements fit in to the overall course and will enable them to identify what they need to do to succeed.

 Learning exercise

Write down one activity that you could use with your students that could be peer assessed. What prompts can you give them to guide and structure their feedback? Is there room for praise in their assessment?

Build confidence and self-esteem

Although confidence and self-esteem generally go hand in hand, there are subtle differences and it may be that the distinction is relevant. Arguably, having confidence will rely on having a sufficient amount of self-esteem, as it is difficult to undertake an activity with assurance if you do not believe in yourself. However, students may perform well at times, while still feeling deep down that they are not as proficient as they would like to be. These are natural doubts, yet they need to be overcome when they affect performance. (Have a look at the concept of growth mindset in Chapter 3.)

Be inclusive

In many ways, inclusion is what we strive for. Effective teachers want their students to learn; they want their students to progress in personal ways that learning can facilitate. They do not want to exclude anyone as they realise that is a failing on their behalf, apart from being a poor moral action. But this is far from straightforward. Consider the following scenario.

 **Scenario**

You have just started teaching today's lesson and after your brief input you have an activity lined up that will involve collaborative learning and some exploration (with you acting as facilitator). One student is disruptive and you know that if he had stayed off again today (as he has done for the last two sessions) things would run smoothly. You try to reason with him but he becomes more disruptive, gaining an audience along the way. Before you read on, jot down two or three strategies that you could use to address this problem.

First, what is happening here? You may not wish this student any ill-feeling but don't beat yourself up for feeling that your class would be much better without him. However, don't hold on to this thought either. It is important to acknowledge your initial feelings. You are human, after all. Now, remember why you came into teaching. You probably came to help people; you may have come to help others achieve what you have achieved and to overcome personal challenges. All your learners are important to you, so knowing them will help you to understand them better and how best to ensure they are included.

There will be a reason why this student acts in this way, and just because the others are seemingly conforming does not mean that they are learning or that they are happy. Talk to the student and try to get some feedback. Are there barriers that you can identify? (You can refer to Chapter 7 on inclusion for help on this.) The purpose of identifying barriers is to support your students, but it can be difficult if these barriers are related to maths or English and the pressure is on for you to embed these skills.

What is needed is a culture of success, backed by a belief that all can achieve.

(Black, 2001, p18)

PGCE (Postgraduate Certificate in Education) students often state that they cannot teach maths (and English, but not as often) and some are fearful of this in their practice, suggesting that they are concerned with exposure. When this is probed, it seems that a lot of emphasis has been placed on features such as times tables and fractions. However, they understand more than they realise. And times tables – although helpful – are hardly the key to deep mathematical understanding, particularly if they have been learned by rote. So the goal here is to demystify. Print and laminate A4 versions of times tables and through using these students will subconsciously commit many of them to memory. More importantly, however, give them a tool to take away and even the most resistant-to-maths students you encounter can be made to feel at ease. The strategy in the learning exercise box is something that many primary school teachers use and it is effective and raises self-esteem.

 Learning exercise

Hold your hands up front of you, fingers extended, palms facing you. Starting on your left thumb as number one, count up to ten as you move from each finger, eventually arriving at your right-hand thumb. This should be number 10. (Be mindful of any students with hands that will alienate them from the exercise.) You are now looking to solve mathematical calculations in the nine times table - anything from one times nine to ten times nine. Using this range of numbers, ask your students for a sum. For example, they say seven times nine. Tell them to bend the finger that corresponds to this number - the seventh finger (the ring finger on the right hand). Then, they count the number of fingers to the left of this (six) and then the number of fingers to the right (three). This gives them six and three so the answer is 63. This is a simple but effective exercise and is fun.

For students who struggle with times tables, this gives them something useful to take away from the lesson and could be the first step in securing their faith in you. Some students believe they will never understand basic numerical concepts and knowing their barriers will help you to facilitate effective learning and will lead to them feeling included in your classroom.

Identify areas for improvement

Barriers can be addressed by giving feedback and setting targets. Feedback is a key component of assessment, particularly if it is dialogic, and it can help your students to self-assess (Gravells, 2016). This is important for self-esteem and can reinforce learning. Many of us dislike criticism – it can make or break us – yet we often wish to know what we can do to improve. This needs to be implemented appropriately, however. If you feel that a student has many areas for development, don't list them all. Instead, focus on two or three main ones they can work on as part of their development. Small steps will be more useful and will help them to eventually overcome their barriers.

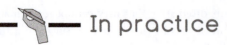

In practice

At 46, Edith returned to learning after many years out of education and enrolled on a hair and beauty course at college. She was encouraged to engage but found it difficult competing with her peers. Moreover, her first piece of work was assessed and contained 72 comments from her tutor, many of which related to grammar and spelling. Edith left college soon after this. She recalls that her tutor was 'obsessed with maths and English'. Feeling she could no longer compete, she tragically claimed, 'that course wasn't for me'.

Build on experience

In addition to wanting to know how they are doing, students often need to be reminded of how far they have travelled.

Learning exercise

Revisit your students' individual learning plans (or devise some if you don't have any) and make a note of one personal goal for each student. What resources can you find to incorporate some of these into one of your sessions? You can refer to Fred's fishing example above for inspiration.

It is important to acknowledge the wealth of experience students bring from both their personal lives and their educational history. However, these experiences will colour their perceptions and may contribute to their barriers to learning. Perhaps due to its clear-cut nature of being either right or wrong, maths is often an obstacle and some students speak of having maths 'gremlins'. In many instances, this is representative of 11 years of problematic schooling and may have resulted in a 'maths isn't for me' attitude. Such barriers are difficult to address and it may be useful to explore the concept of growth mindset (see Chapter 3).

Moreover, rumours of 'failing to achieve as a left-brain thinker' may abound as the lateralisation of brain function is exaggerated, whereupon some students may believe that they are either strong in English or maths – but not both. Therefore, part of your role as a good teacher will be to develop the students' capacity to excel in these areas against these odds and to shut out any misconceptions of 'leave maths to the left-brain thinkers'. Your students may need to realise that when they are learning, *both* sides of their brain will be used, regardless of what they are studying. In other words, allowing the brain to function as a whole (as it will do anyway), and acknowledging that we all have the potential to excel in both maths and English, will contribute towards a better attitude to learning.

> *If I had to reduce all of educational psychology to just one principle, I would say this: The most important single factor influencing learning is what the learner already knows.*
>
> (Ausubel, 1968, pvi)

In many ways, embedding maths and English will help your students beyond the classroom as they become more autonomous and aware of their potential. Maths and English affect our everyday lives and it is these opportunities that you will be looking to capitalise on in order to add relevance to the students' learning. For instance, in addition to the obvious use of maths and English when shopping – calculating prices of two-for-one offers, deciphering complex signage and so on – some of your students will be interested in mortgages and you can run an extra-curricular session on this with maths and English built in, perhaps focusing on strategies for calculating percentages and for understanding ratio.

When building on experience, Bruner's concept of the spiral curriculum is useful for reaffirming ideas and for developing learning. The concept allows for the extended exploration of a topic over time, with each occasion requiring more depth of understanding. Consider the following scenario.

 Scenario

You are looking to lay laminate flooring in your house throughout. You will need to calculate the area and perimeter of each room and then use these measurements to decide on how much materials you will need.

The knowledge needed to undertake this activity is in some ways transferable to other situations, such as laying a lawn in a garden, wallpapering a room, or fitting beds into a hospital ward. In the spiral curriculum, however, we don't just return to area and perimeter. We raise the complexity to develop the students' understanding of the strategies and to contextualise the skills within other problems.

When calculating area and perimeter, you need to consider features of the room such as a chimney breast, a fireplace, an oven, a built-in wardrobe, or other specialist furniture items where the flooring would not go underneath.

The students can draw on their existing knowledge, yet be challenged to think about what they are doing in order to learn more effectively (Coe *et al.*, 2014). To go further, we can encourage more complex thinking by introducing further calculations for purchasing the laminate flooring, such as the following:

- Buy two packs and get a third free (ratio).

- Wednesday is 15 per cent off day (percentages).

- Join up for a store card and get five pound back on every £50 spent today (ratio and deduction).

- An odd number of boards are needed, yet each pack contains ten boards (estimation and decision-making).

The spiral curriculum, then, acts as a foundation for building on and can be a slow-release mechanism for introducing complex calculations.

Chapter summary

Incorporating maths and English in your teaching is about identifying barriers - particularly where students have already studied these subjects at school - and getting to know your students so that you can find appropriate ways to motivate them. Are your learning activities relevant? Are they meaningful?

This chapter has supported you to:

- Get to know your students.
- Identify aspects of English and maths and emphasise what your students can do.
- Build on students' strengths and utilise their ambitions and personal interests.
- Support and praise.
- Build confidence and self-esteem.
- Be inclusive.
- Identify areas for improvement.
- Build on experience.

Further reading

Sharrock, T (2016) *Embedding English and Maths: Practical Strategies for FE and Post-16 Tutors*. Northwich: Critical Publishing.

References

Ausubel, DP (1968) *Educational Psychology: A Cognitive View*. New York: Holt, Rinehart and Winston Inc.

Black, P (2001) Formative assessment and curriculum consequences, in Scott, D (ed) *Curriculum and Assessment*. London: Greenwood Publishing Group.

Coe, R, Aloisi, C, Higgins, S and Major, LE (2014) *What Makes Great Teaching? Review of the Underpinning Research*. Available at: http://www.suttontrust.com/wp-content/uploads/2014/10/What-Makes-Great-Teaching-REPORT.pdf.

Gravells, A (2016) *Principles and Practices of Assessment*. London: Sage/Learning Matters.

Useful websites

BBC Bitesize – **www.bbc.co.uk/education/**

BBC Skillswise – **www.bbc.co.uk/skillswise/0/**

BKSB – **www.bksb.co.uk/**

Education and Training Foundation – **www.et-foundation.co.uk/**

English teaching advice – **https://community.tes.com/forums/english.14/**

Foundation Online Learning – **www.foundationonline.org.uk/**

Functional skills – **www.forskills.co.uk/what-are-functional-skills/**

Maths and English support – **www.maths-english.com/**

Maths teaching advice – **https://community.tes.com/forums/mathematics.25/**

TES resources – **www.tes.com/teaching-resources**

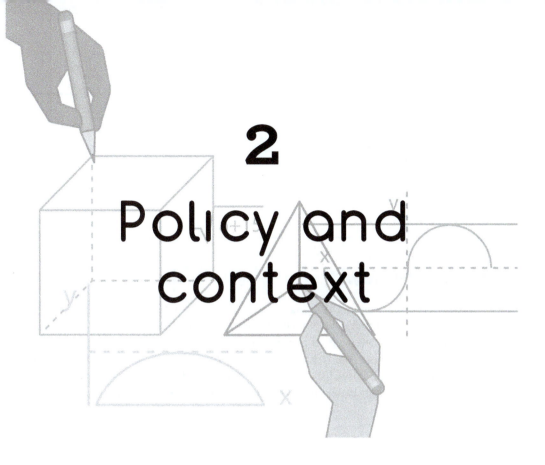

2
Policy and context

 ── This chapter ──

This chapter explores policy concerns of English and maths in recent years and illustrates some of the changes that have impacted on teaching and learning in the sector, such as the need for all 16–19-year-olds to continue to work towards a minimum requirement, and the implications this has for many vocational teachers. For instance, in the Further Education and Skills Inspection handbook of 2016 (Ofsted, 2016, p45), the Ofsted framework for FE states that providers will be judged inadequate (grade 4) *if their students are not developing English, mathematics, ICT or employability skills adequately to equip them for their future progression.*

This chapter will support you to understand:

- Where are we now?
- The international scene.
- Policy overview.
- The Wolf report.
- Employability.
- Apprenticeships and vocational learning.

(Continued)

(Continued)

- Vocational versus academic.
- Key factors for embedment.
- The future and functional skills.
- 2014 professional standards for teachers and trainers in England.
- Implications for teaching.

Where are we now?

Over the last twenty years, maths and English have consistently featured as important areas for both personal and professional development. In particular, maths has been linked to economic success and has become a key segment of the emblem of good education throughout the world. For example, an international comparison of maths over the last decade has regularly positioned England in the mid- to high-20s (CBI, 2014) and this has raised many policy concerns. Moreover, according to the Independent Panel on Technical Education (IPTE, 2016, p8), the system needs a major overhaul.

> [T]here are serious problems with the existing system. In particular, it is overcomplex and fails to provide the skills most needed for the 21st century. By 2020, the UK is set to fall to 28th out of 33 OECD countries in terms of developing intermediate skills, and the size of the post-secondary technical education sector in England is extremely small by international standards. This adversely affects our productivity, where we lag behind competitors like Germany and France by as much as 36 percentage points.

In the government's latest (at the time of writing) statistical first release, it was claimed, *Attainment of Level 2 (GCSE A*–C or other Level 2 qualifications) in English and maths by age 19 rose from 67.8 per cent in 2014 to 70.0 per cent in 2015* (DfE, 2016). However, the missing 30 per cent suggests there is still much work to be done if policy requirements are to be appeased. Another major concern is that such young people who are lacking in guidance and support will likely become NEET (not in education, employment or training) and may even resort to crime, having become disaffected with society.

Moreover, despite much policy focus on building skills and raising standards to level 2 and beyond, in order to develop the nation's financial standing, Finlay et al. (2007) suggest that an overall increase in the standard of skills does not necessarily lead to a growth in the economy. What is clear, however, is that government policy – a major driving force in education (and holder of ye education purse strings) – is adamant in its quest for much greater nationwide ability in English and maths, and this affects teachers.

Learning exercise

Make a note of the policies in your institution that you feel will be of particular relevance to your teaching/embedding of English and maths in the coming year.

In 2014, the government introduced a requirement wherein all post-16 students who have not achieved at least a grade C in GCSE English and maths will continue studying these subjects, with the maximum time allowed being until they are 19. However, this does mean that, having started at 14, some students may be studying these subjects for up to five years; therefore, some of your 18-year-olds may be significantly less motivated than expected and this is an area where you will need to pick up the pieces. Furthermore, it is most likely you will be expected to teach maths and English so it may be in your interest to upskill too, if necessary, as the FE sector is clearly heading in this direction. Millions of pounds have been invested in bursaries *to attract good graduates into teaching* English and maths, and to support existing teachers wishing to develop their skills (Kuczera *et al.*, 2016, p31).

The international scene

The English government's aim for maths and English is for a minimum of level 2 across the country, although GCSE achievement at grades A*–C in these areas is their *preferred measure of successful secondary education* (DBIS, 2012, p14). International comparisons with more than 60 countries are made every few years through TIMSS (Trends in International Mathematics and Science Study) and PIRLS (Progress in International Reading Literacy Study). The most recent TIMMS (2015) suggested that the top five countries – Singapore, Hong Kong SAR, Korea, Chinese Taipei and Japan – have a 20-year edge on all other participating countries (Mullis *et al.*, 2016), with England sitting in tenth place. Criticisms of TIMSS suggest that as it is curriculum-based, it is therefore dependent on the coverage of specific criteria in the chosen years. For FE, a perhaps more relevant international assessment is the Program for International Student Assessment (PISA) as this is drawn from reading, mathematics and science, and, to a lesser extent, the problem solving and financial literacy of 15-year-olds.

Again, the comparability of this type of testing has been disputed, such as identifying the problematic nature of cultural variables when measuring real-life contexts (Sjøberg, 2012), but these figures are used to fuel policymaking. The latest PISA (OECD, 2016) shows that although England is comparatively above average, it has merely sustained its average reading and mathematics score since 2006, despite many efforts to raise the game. However, in a report for the Department for Education, Jerrim and Shure (2016, p6) note that *the relatively poor mathematics skills of England's low-achieving pupils stands out as a weakness of England's education system*. Thus, from a social justice perspective, there is an achievement gap that needs to be addressed.

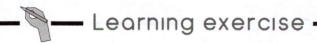 Learning exercise

Using a cohort of learners you regularly teach, identify the top five barriers in relation to English and maths. What can you do to overcome some of these?

Policy overview

The focus on the nation's ability in mathematics and the need for FE to feed into employment and life skills is both current and highly relevant, albeit the momentum is far from new. In 1982, for instance, the Cockcroft report (1982, np) stated that, *Few subjects in the school curriculum are as important to the future of the nation as mathematics*. The report also identified *the hesitant grasp many adults have of even quite simple mathematical skills*. Move 32 years on and an unfortunately similar scenario is depicted: *Every other country in the developed world concentrates on improving the language and mathematics skills of its post-16 vocational students, and so, belatedly, should England* (Wolf, 2011, p11). Indeed, despite years of varying emphasis on maths and English, we remain in a situation where *improving post-16 provision is a matter of urgency* (Wolf, 2011, p85).

> *Literacy, numeracy, communication and information technology, together with problem-solving skills and effective team-working, are widely recognised as key skills for employment.*
>
> (Kennedy, 1997, p17)

In the early 1990s, FE was undergoing major changes. Building on the earlier white paper of 1988 (Employment for the 1990s) that looked at employment prospects, the Further and Higher Education Act 1992 further developed the thinking that sectoral competition was a healthy way to progress and to raise standards. Such changes resulted in *two new funding streams for 16 to 19 and adult further education* which were heavily focused on outcomes (Panchamia, 2012, p2). Funding for training and work-based learning fell within the remit of Training and Enterprise Councils (TECs), while the Further Education Funding Council (FEFC) financed FE. This neoliberal approach to education has persisted and has perpetuated the discourse of 'raising standards' that has permeated education in England. Understandably, part of this lay in the government's principal concern of ensuring *everyone had the basic numeracy and literacy skills … they needed to access employment* (Panchamia, 2012, p2). However, such drives can often have a backlash on the arts and creativity and, ironically, vocational teachers are now being called upon to be more creative in order to embed skills in maths and English, despite many not having such skills themselves (LSIS, 2013).

In 1999, the Moser report (Moser, 1999) quantified illiteracy and innumeracy in adults as one in five. With an estimated population of 59.5 million at the time (see **www.populstat.info**), this equates to around 11.9 million people. It suggested a major rethinking of policy aims for education was needed. Somewhere along the compulsory education system, many people were being failed (were failing?). It was claimed that many adults did not have basic skills in literacy and numeracy, such as reading a Yellow Pages (What's a Yellow Pages?, the Google natives cry) or calculating the area of a floor, even with a calculator. This led to the *skills for life* strategy, aimed at targeting the (what were previously termed) basic skills of literacy and numeracy that people needed to function in society. In 2001, the Department for Education and Skills proposed that the skills for life agenda should improve the basic skills of around three-quarters of a million adults by 2004 – a goal which, seemingly, was comfortably reached in time (DfES, 2004).

 ── Learning exercise ──────────

Familiarise yourself with your institution's procedure for assessing and recording students' levels in maths and English. For example, BKSB (Basic Key Skills Builder, **www.bksb.co.uk/**) is popular with many colleges. How often are the students assessed?

In 2006, the Leitch (2006, p2) report recommended a target for the UK for 2020, for 95 per cent of adults to have achieved *the basic skills of functional literacy and numeracy*. An ambitious target indeed, but one that has driven policy ever since. The report noted that *7 million adults lack functional numeracy and 5 million lack functional literacy* (Leitch, 2006, p10). This shows an improvement on the suggested figures of 1999, but obviously is still representative of a nationwide concern. However, a major problem with the education system in England – as noted in the Wolf report – is that there are far too many qualifications available and this causes problems for student progression through poor standardisation, and/or differing levels of quality. Wolf (2011, p84) exemplifies this through her identification of the previous literacy and numeracy equivalent qualifications.

Millions of key skills certificates have been awarded in 'application of number' and communication', as the key skill maths and English tests are known. These awards contributed directly to one of the previous government's most important targets, and were very easy to pass, which is extremely important in a funding system which pays partly by results.

Indeed, Wolf also alludes to the online test for English in key skills which involved no writing whatsoever, as it was mostly multiple choice.

Furthermore, the IPTE (2016, p11) reports that, *In September 2015, there were over 21,000 qualifications on Ofqual's Register of Regulated Qualifications, offered by 158 different awarding organisations. Individuals aiming for a future in plumbing, for example, have to choose between 33 qualifications.* In many ways, then, technical qualifications have become embroiled in a process of marketisation, wherein a competitive, but not necessarily quality-driven, system has resulted in many 16–19-year-olds having to make difficult choices. Thus, it appears that in some respects little has changed since the Wolf report of 2011 and although this is still a relatively recent report, with cohorts of around one and a half to two million 16–18-year-olds in England each year, this has the potential to impact on many, many lives.

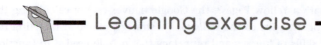

Learning exercise

Visit the government's website below and identify any reforms to GCSEs that could affect your teaching:

www.gov.uk/government/collections/reform-of-gcse-qualifications-by-ofqual

The Wolf report

Professor Alison Wolf's review of vocational education in 2011 suggested that some young people in Key Stage 4 (14–16) of their compulsory education should be encouraged to undertake high-quality vocational provision in the FE sector. As a result, from September 2013, FE and sixth-form colleges have been legally entitled to enrol 14–16-year-olds on vocational courses in addition to their statutory curriculum areas, such as English and maths. Although young people at 14+ have been in a position to access FE for many years (the Further and Higher Education Act 1992 laid out guidelines for what was allowed), this opportunity has long been dominated by reactive thinking, as colleges have for many years worked collaboratively with schools and local authorities in allocating placements for those considered to be disaffected (Allan, 2014; Lumby, 2012). However, the amended arrangement means that colleges are now in a position to directly recruit and can thus access funding for doing so. The implications for teachers are wide and the importance of English and maths teaching and embedding will undoubtedly be sustained for many years to come.

Employability

It has been argued, numerous times, that literacy and numeracy skills are fundamental aspects of employment. Indeed, Moser (1999) suggests that poor levels result in individuals illustrating lower work productivity, ill-health, disaffection and social exclusion. Therefore, it has been found that employers actively seek English and maths skills when recruiting and when processing applications for interview. However, Wolf's assessment of FE in 2011 resulted in a searing indictment of England's ability to develop efficacious employability through its existing qualifications: *The staple offer for between a quarter and a third of the post-16 cohort is a diet of low-level vocational qualifications, most of which have little to no labour market value* (Wolf, 2011, p7). As such, the diagnosis called for a major overhaul of the system.

> *Most countries across Europe and other advanced economies have experienced an alarming rise in the numbers of young people (aged between 16 and 24 years) who are detached from both the labour market and the education and training system in recent years.*
>
> (Maguire, 2015, p122)

A review by the Education and Training Foundation in 2015 looked at perceptions of maths and English and found that although employers trust GCSEs, they are more *concerned about the maths and English skills of their recruits* (ETF, 2015, p3). Their focus was on functional skills which may be embedded within vocational areas or operate as stand-alone qualifications. Functional skills (FS) were officially introduced in the 2009/10 academic year (ETF, 2015), although they had been piloted in several regions prior to this. Generally, employers regard FS as important qualifications, particularly beyond 19 years of age, where it is no longer compulsory to work towards GCSE. The ETF report suggests there is a wide perception that these are stepping-stone qualifications towards GCSE – in much the same way the Cambridge Progression units operate – although they were not designed that way. However, employers feel that they should act as an alternative route to the GCSE, particularly as there is a focus on life and work. In FS, maths is embedded in real-life contexts in order to establish skills that can be reconstructed elsewhere, whereas GCSEs have been traditionally more generic, drawing on skills that are mostly academic and aligned with further study. However, with recent reforms the landscape is changing.

Apprenticeships and vocational learning

In recent years, apprenticeships have taken on a new shape and in response to some key reviews on vocational education – Wolf (2011), Richard (2012), LSIS (2013) and UKCES (2013) – the Department for Business, Innovation and Skills (DBIS, 2014, p6) has refocused a significant aspect of their design and validation on employers. As such, employers can, *Identify those qualifications in maths and English which best enable adult learners to progress to GCSE standard.* According to the Richard review (2012), *Apprenticeships should attract some of the best students, including those who have already excelled in maths and English at school.* Clearly, then, there is a need to change the perception of apprenticeships and perhaps even a move towards generating parity of esteem between academic and vocational learning, as well as developing stronger links with the world of employment.

Vocational versus academic

Despite decades of developing work-related programmes, vocational learning still has a long way to go to achieve the status of academic learning. Many so-called vocational learning activities, however, are underpinned by rigorous theoretical knowledge, acquired and devised as a result of robust academic research. Brain surgery, for instance (see Robbie's case study in Chapter 11), could be categorised as *vocational* and draws on an extremely high level of tactile ability.

It has long been government motivation to address this concern and the *14–19 Diplomas,* introduced around 2008 (and killed off around 2013), aimed to achieve this. The premise has been noted many times and to combat this the 1996 Tomlinson report recommended that all 14–19 qualifications fall under a single framework. However, recent recommendations for two post-16 routes, one *technical* and one *academic* (IPTE, 2016), might sustain the negative, and misconceived, belief by some that individuals are either good with their heads or good with their hands and should choose a route that is appropriate.

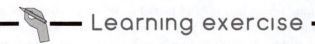

Learning exercise

In relation to maths and English teaching, identify three training needs you feel will help you to develop in your role over the coming year.

Key factors for embedment

Recent research by NIACE (Robey and Jones, 2015), commissioned by the Education and Training Foundation, explored why some students were leaving school without the benchmark A*–C in maths and/or English. They identify ten key messages for the sector that can impact on attitudes to learning, three of which are particularly relevant to embedding these skills:

- *Learning is **fun**, **interactive** and **practical**;*

- *There is a strong understanding of the **purpose** and importance of holding these qualifications, relating them to real-life situations;*

- *Learning has a personal **relevance** which is explained to learners and feedback on their performance relates the activities to the qualification they are studying for.*

(Robey and Jones, 2015, p7)

Although the bold font is in the original document, the terms are particularly relevant to the argument in this book. Learning that is fun will be engaging and will stimulate interest and embed needs to illustrate relevance to create a purpose for your students to continue. This is essential if you wish to sustain motivation.

The points are helpful because they come from the learners. Students in FE report that they particularly like the environment because it is generally relaxed, informal and flexible, where both students and tutors can illustrate mutual respect (Hurry *et al.*, 2005).

The final recommendation is to capture a student voice and this is to be encouraged as it can help to identify a mismatch between your perceptions and those of your students. A student voice can open up avenues of unexplored motivation and stimuli that you can draw on to improve your teaching and this ties in with metacognition, as it encourages individuals to be reflective and self-critical – factors that can empower your students.

In Britain, it is 'cool' not to be able to understand mathematics. Adults have been so 'turned off' mathematics in school that they are happy to boast that they don't understand it and don't need it.

(Tall, 2008, p6)

Individuals who have previously been marginalised by the education system often respond positively to an FE environment, particularly when it is perceived as an opportunity for a fresh start. In some instances, many years of compulsory schooling has led to disaffection, negative attitudes towards learning, and often anxiety and even fear. With this in mind, your role is to build the bridge between you and your learners and possibly reconnect these learners to earlier experiences, before they switched off. For many, returning to education is daunting and potentially reminiscent of bad times; therefore, you will need to help your students to reconceptualise learning and regain their motivation, enthusiasm and, most importantly, confidence and self-esteem. This is no easy task and may take months of painstaking groundwork, but it will be worthwhile once you have witnessed the effect you can have on somebody's life.

The future and functional skills

Reviews carried out by ETF (2015) and Ofqual (2014) found that a great majority of employers and training providers believe that functional skills are relevant to work and life. Thus, there is currently a focus on ensuring that all teachers have the necessary skills to teach maths and English. However, the ETF report (2015) suggests that many English and maths teachers are struggling to relate their subject to some vocational areas, whilst some vocational teachers don't feel they have the underpinning skills to support students in English and maths. In some ways, then, a stand-off exists and colleges are encouraging more collaboration, joint planning and resource sharing (not a bad thing). One strategy could be to network with other institutions to share concerns and to reduce individual workloads.

 Learning exercise

Using the link below, have a look at the Education and Training Foundation's Teach Too programme and note down any ideas for strategies that you could recommend for your setting. Could you approach your mentor/senior manager with these? Is your institution already doing something similar? How is it different?

www.et-foundation.co.uk/supporting/support-for-employers/teach/

Although the Wolf report (2011, p84) claimed that FS were *not in themselves an adequate 'maths and English' diet for the 16–19 cohort* – and the view that there are conceptual problems and standardisation concerns is arguably correct – they have proven extremely popular with employers. Moreover, given that employers are now more at liberty to suggest which qualifications apprentices should follow, and that FS are undergoing major changes for standardisation, it is likely that their presence will continue to grow.

Indeed, the functional nature of these qualifications holds much appeal. For instance, from September 2015, GCSEs in maths and English were revised to become more applicable to everyday situations, involving problem solving in real-life scenarios, and grammar and spelling were linked to their potential usefulness outside the classroom. As such, FS are arguably attempting to be the epitome of embedment and if they are not deemed to be a GCSE equivalent as they stand, their imminent overhaul may see that they are a competitive force to be reckoned with as they appear to have much staying power.

The need for a level 3 qualification in FS has been raised by employers (amongst other people) and this is arguably valid for those studying vocational areas at level 3 and beyond. Indeed, there appears to be a closed focus in relation to English and maths and while students demonstrate skills at level 3 within their vocation, the level of accompanying maths and English should be recognised and validated. However, it is perhaps difficult to design a level 3 qualification where expectations are that, *It would only have currency if there were recognition of its value by employers* (ETF, 2015, p15), particularly where *employers are not experts in either subject and do not understand in any detail skills and knowledge covered in qualifications* (ETF, 2015, p10).

 Learning exercise

Find out which examining boards your institution uses for its functional skills qualification and/or English and maths GCSEs. Make a note of these and visit the websites to familiarise yourself with their requirements.

2014 professional standards for teachers and trainers in England

In 2012, Lord Lingfield's review proposed that teachers in the FE and skills sector were no longer required to work towards qualified teaching and learning status (QTLS); however, those who teach maths and/or English and/or provide support for students with SEND (special educational needs and disabilities) are encouraged to attain specialist training. Subsequently, professionalism in the sector began to adopt an alternative approach and part of this reform led to the introduction of the 2014 professional standards, launched by the Education and Training Foundation. As part of the Professional Skills section, teachers are expected to, *Address the mathematics and English needs of learners and work creatively to overcome individual barriers to learning* (**www.et-foundation.co.uk**).

The standards were designed to support teaching in the sector and aim to model *good practice* and to help teachers address gaps in their knowledge and skills. The Education and Training Foundation (ETF) website outlines the intended audience:

- *Teachers and trainers of post-16 learners working in further education colleges (excluding sixth-form colleges), the community, commercial and charitable organisations, industry, the armed and uniformed services, prisons/offender learning and other public sector organisations*

- *Their employers*

(www.et-foundation.co.uk/professional-standards-review/)

According to the website, the standards *define the professional requirements of teachers, trainers and tutors of post 16 learners, and underpin good teaching practice in the sector* (**www.et-foundation.co.uk**). Perhaps one of the most effective aspects is that they facilitate reflection and self-assessment of professional development needs. According to the ETF, the standards need to become the property of the profession and as such have been scrutinised by key figures in the field to encourage a grassroots approach to policymaking.

Learning exercise

Consider the policies referred to in this chapter and think about the current drive to embed English and maths. Is the situation likely to change in the next two to five years? If yes, how will it change? If no, why won't it change?

Implications for teaching

From August 2015, the 'stepping stone' qualifications were omitted from the condition of funding. However, this amendment does not apply to apprenticeships and other job-related training where functional skills can still be studied. Maths and English GCSEs have also been revised and September 2016 saw the new ones get underway. These are substantial changes for the FE sector and ones that will undoubtedly impact on you as a teacher. Whatever you teach, the condition of funding will ensure that, where appropriate, your 16–19-year-olds are undertaking maths and English and you may well be called on to support this within your own subject.

Policy pressures, then, will filter through to practice (as with most areas of education) but developing students' literacies is an arguably important aspect of social justice, as you can empower your students. Knowledge is power, as the old adage suggests, and a lack of knowledge is certainly disempowering for many, as can be seen by Pierre Bourdieu's notion of capital (Jenkins, 2006).

In education, policy carries a lot of power – some good, some not so good – but this does not mean that as a teacher you are limited in what you can change. If nothing else, you are changing lives – a major feat in itself – and this ensures that teaching is, on the whole, a worthwhile exercise and a reputable profession. The current policy focus on English and maths, then, is arguably a positive feature of learners' development and your role is to utilise it wisely.

If 'English and maths' is not your forte, don't be disillusioned. We all have the capacity to learn and barriers are often based on attitude, personality and self-esteem, rather than actual ability. The concept of 'you can't teach an old dog new tricks' has been robustly challenged in neuroscience research and new neuronal pathways are generated through learning. As such, you should challenge misconceptions and tackle your own maths and/or English gremlins.

Chapter summary

This chapter has supported you to understand:

- Where are we now?
- The international scene.
- Policy overview.

(Continued)

(Continued)

- The Wolf report.
- Employability.
- Apprenticeships and vocational learning.
- Vocational versus academic.
- Key factors for embedment.
- The future and functional skills.
- 2014 professional standards for teachers and trainers in England.
- Implications for teaching.

References

Allan, D (2014) Dealing with disaffection: the influence of work-based learning on 14–16-year-old students' attitudes to school, *Empirical Research in Vocational Education and Training*, 6(10): 1–18.

CBI (2014) *Gateway to Growth: CBI/Pearson Education and Skills Survey*. London: Pearson.

Cockcroft, WH (1982) *Mathematics Counts: Report of the Committee of Inquiry into the Teaching of Mathematics in Schools under the Chairmanship of Dr WH Cockcroft*. London: Her Majesty's Stationery Office. Available at: **www.educationengland.org.uk/documents/cockcroft/cockcroft1982. html#04**.

DBIS [Department for Business, Innovation and Skills] (2012) *Professionalism in Further Education: Final Report of the Independent Review Panel*. London: Department for Business, Innovation and Skills.

DBIS (2014) *Getting the Job Done*. London: Department for Business, Innovation and Skills.

DfE (2016) *Level 2 and 3 Attainment in England: Attainment by Age 19 in 2015*. SFR 12/2016, Department for Education. Available at: **www.gov.uk/government/uploads/system/uploads/attachment_ data/file/514296/SFR12_2016.pdf**.

DfES [Department for Education and Skills] (2004) *Skills for Life: The National Strategy for Improving Adult Literacy and Numeracy Skills*. London: Department for Education and Skills.

ETF [Education and Training Foundation] (2015) *Making Maths and English Work for All – March 2015*. The Education and Training Foundation. Available at: **www.et-foundation.co.uk/wp-content/ uploads/2015/03/Making-maths-and-English-work-for-all-25_03_2015001.pdf**.

Finlay, I, Spours, K, Steer, R, Coffield, F, Gregson, M, and Hodgson, A (2007) The heart of what we do: policies on teaching, learning and assessment in the new learning and skills sector, *Journal of Vocational Education and Training*, 59(2): 137–53.

Hurry, J, Brazier, L, Snapes, K and Wilson, A (2005) *Improving the Literacy and Numeracy of Disaffected Young People in Custody and in the Community*. London: NRDC.

IPTE [Independent Panel on Technical Education] (2016) *Report of the Independent Panel on Technical Education*. London: DfE.

Jenkins, R (2006) *Pierre Bourdieu.* London: Taylor & Francis.

Jerrim, J and Shure, N (2016) *Achievement of 15-Year-Olds in England: PISA 2015 National Report.* London: UCL, Institute of Education.

Kennedy, H (1997) *Learning Works: Widening Participation in Further Education.* Coventry: The Further Education Funding Council.

Kuczera, M, Field, S and Windisch, HC (2016) *Building Skills for All: A Review of England.* Paris: OECD Publishing.

Leitch (2006) *Prosperity for All in the Global Economy: World Class Skills.* Norwich: HMSO.

LSIS (2013) *It's about work … Excellent Adult Vocational Teaching and Learning.* London: Learning and Skills Improvement Service.

Lumby, J (2012) Disengaged and disaffected young people: surviving the system, *British Educational Research Journal*, 38(2): 261–79.

Maguire, S (2015) NEET, unemployed, inactive or unknown: why does it matter?, *Educational Research*, 57(2): 121–32.

Moser, C (1999) *Improving Literacy and Numeracy: A Fresh Start.* The report of the working group chaired by Sir Claus Moser on behalf of the Department for Education and Skills. Available at: **www.life longlearning.co.uk/mosergroup/index**.

Mullis, IVS, Martin, MO, Foy, P and Hooper, M (2016) *TIMSS 2015 International Results in Mathematics.* Available at: **http://timssandpirls.bc.edu/timss2015/international-results/**.

OECD (2016) *PISA 2015 Results (Volume I): Excellence and Equity in Education.* Paris: OECD Publishing. Available at: **http://dx.doi.org/10.1787/9789264266490-en**.

Ofqual (2014) *Improving Functional Skills Qualifications.* Coventry: Office of Qualifications and Examinations Regulation.

Ofsted (2016) *Further Education and Skills Inspection Handbook.* Manchester: The Office for Standards in Education. Available at: **www.gov.uk/government/uploads/system/uploads/ attachment_data/file/553864/Further_education_and_skills_inspection_handbook_ for_use_from_September_2016.pdf**.

Panchamia, N (2012) *Choice and Competition in Further Education.* Available at: **www.institutefor government.org.uk/sites/default/files/publications/FE%20Briefing%20final.pdf**.

Richard, D (2012) *Richard Review of Apprenticeships.* London: DBIS.

Robey, C and Jones, E (2015) *Engaging Learners in GCSE Maths and English.* Leicester: National Institute of Adult Continuing Education (England and Wales).

Sjøberg, S (2012) PISA: politics, fundamental problems and intriguing results, *Recherches en Education*, (14): 1–21.

Tall, D (2008) Using Japanese lesson study in teaching mathematics, *The Scottish Mathematical Council Journal*, 38: 45–50.

TIMMS (2015) TIMSS 2015 and TIMSS Advanced 2015 International Results. Available at: **http:// timss2015.org/#/?playlistId=0&videoId=0**.

UKCES (2013) *Review of Adult Vocational Qualifications*. London: UK Commission for Employment and Skills.

Wolf, A (2011) *Review of Vocational Education: The Wolf Report*. London: DfE.

━━━ Useful websites ━━━

Department for Education – **www.gov.uk/**

Education and Training Foundation – **www.et-foundation.co.uk/**

FE advice – **www.feadvice.org.uk/**

PIRLS – **http://timssandpirls.bc.edu/**

PISA – **www.oecd-ilibrary.org/**

Population statistics – **www.populstat.info**

Reform of GCSE qualifications by Ofqual – **www.gov.uk/government/collections/reform-of-gcse-qualifications-by-ofqual**

TIMSS – **http://timss2015.org/**

3
Theories on, and around, learning

 This chapter

This chapter introduces the reader to theories of learning. However, due to the large number of theories available (several books could easily be written to cover these), it is purposefully selective in its approach. As such, it acts as a springboard for further exploration and aims to highlight the potentially rich experience that can be achieved through drawing on theory and research. A list of suggested texts for further reading is available at the end.

This chapter will explore:

- What do we know?
- Why use theory?
- Whistle-stop tour of behaviourism.
- Early behaviourism.
- Modern behaviourism.
- Thinking about learning: moving beyond the lab rats.
- Assessing understanding.
- The spiral curriculum.
- Getting your students in the zone.

(Continued)

(Continued)

- Representing meaning.
- Humanism.
- How can I use humanism in my teaching?
- Sociocultural approaches and situated learning.
- Learning domains.
- Mindsets.
- Action research.
- Context: author's perspective.

What do we know?

It is important to note from the outset that we do not actually understand the full process of learning as yet, which is why we have theories of course, but this in itself is an attraction for those hungry to explore. According to Olson and Hergenhahn (2016, p15), *Because a theory is merely a research tool, it cannot be right or wrong; it is either useful or it is not useful.* This means that there is much scope to experiment, to generate new methods of teaching and, potentially, to discover more effective ways to learn. Established theories are based on much observation and research and as such can contribute to our understanding of how teaching impacts on students, and how we can adapt such teaching to enable a more efficient learning process.

Why use theory?

The theoretical approaches in this chapter have been chosen because they are related to many teacher education programmes in England and thus provide a useful complement to professional practice. It is important to consider how theory plays a significant role in teaching and, in particular, your maths and English teaching. The extent to which you engage with these theories will depend on what resonates with your teaching and on your further reading. This process is actively encouraged because it is what generates new knowledge – always challenge and interrogate yourself, your teaching and your thinking. In the same manner in which you would stretch and challenge your learners, stretch and challenge yourself and build theory into your teaching.

In the wonderful world of education, you will be dealing with humans (hopefully) and not robots (depending on the shelf life of this book, of course, and your subject) and you will find that they are as complex as it gets. The brain is a fascinating machine – if we may call it one – and humans understand comparatively little of its functioning. So, theory is very much in its infancy and will remain so until we better understand how and why we behave, how and why we learn, and what can be effective in developing our understanding. Even then, the individual nature of meaning and interpretation, and thus learning, may never be completely understood. Having said this, what we do have is both fascinating and arguably useful for teaching and neuroscience has progressed hugely in recent years. Theories can inform practice and the two are heavily intertwined; therefore, it is likely that you will take many enlightening ideas from exploring them which will stimulate your thinking.

Learning exercise

Make a note of the top two theories (or strategies) you have heard through either your practice or your teaching course. Can you write one line of explanation for each?

Whistle-stop tour of behaviourism

Behaviourists believe that when learning occurs we see a change in a person's behaviour and that teaching can contribute to such change. The use of a stimulus often acts as a reward and is used to produce a specific outcome; thus, controlling this process could mean that students can be guided towards acting in the way the teacher wishes them to. Alternatively, the stimulus could be negative, such as a punishment, but the basic premise remains and the expected behaviour is a response to this. Some aspects of behaviourism are clearly useful for teaching, such as strategies for dealing with disruptions or for tackling disaffection. However, these strategies are general and there is obviously no guarantee that they will work with everyone.

Here is how behaviourism could work: a teacher sets homework and those who complete it can have a reward (something coveted by the students). Those who don't complete the homework have to complete it over lunch. The positive stimulus is the reward and the negative stimulus is working through lunch, but the expected outcome is the same. Whether the students want the reward or do not want the punishment (or both), they should produce the homework. The theory holds that if the stimulus is strong enough, the response will be that which the teacher desires. Of course, there are variables to consider and the concept has been challenged for a number of reasons.

Early behaviourism

Edward Thorndike (1874–1949) experimented with a cat in a box and looked at ways in which the cat could be trained to escape. He concluded that the cat 'learned' the escape route because it could repeat the action. Thorndike's *Law of Effect* suggests that if behaviour leads to a reward it will be continued, whereas if it doesn't then that behaviour will be discontinued. Despite this early work (and others before him), it was John Broadus Watson (1878–1958), and then Burrhus Frederic Skinner (1904–1990), who gained much more credit for behaviourism as they popularised it. Watson 'progressed' his research to humans, with *Little Albert* involved in horrendous, unethical experimentation. Albert was conditioned to respond to a stimulus – a loud noise combined with the sight of an animal – to prompt a change in behaviour as he associated the animal with the fear and anxiety that the noise instilled. Skinner observed how a trapped rat 'learned' to press a lever to release food. Mostly through discovery, the rat stumbles upon the lever and then repeats the behaviour when it realises that this action is followed by a reward. Skinner called this *operant conditioning* and his work builds on earlier research, such as Thorndike's cat and Pavlov's dogs.

Ivan Pavlov (1849–1936) won the Nobel Prize in 1904 for gleaning an understanding of how dogs respond to a stimulus. Unlike the later work of Skinner, the reaction was part of our automaticity and thus uncontrolled and was termed *classical conditioning*. For Pavlov, dogs salivating at the sight of food prompted his thinking into stimulating this process in other ways and he *conditioned* the dogs through association. A bell was rung every time food was presented and the dogs eventually associated the bell with eating. Consequently, merely ringing the bell led to salivation.

As a concept, this initially appears difficult to use in teaching (at least ethically), but if we consider some types of anxiety and fear as uncontrolled responses it may be useful. For instance, do you have a student that runs out of the classroom when you mention the word maths? Could you introduce a positive stimulus whereupon your students re-associate this concept with something different? Skinner's *operant conditioning* differs in that it is a response we can control. Thus, it is believed that humans could be encouraged to change their responses both automatically and consciously.

Modern behaviourism

So, how does behaviourism fare today? Well, aspects of it are still strong. Consider the use of reinforcement: praising wanted behaviour and deterring unwanted behaviour (Petty, 2014). Behaviourism is also noted as useful for students who require specific guidance or need to follow procedures, or *in environments where there are health hazards* (Bates, 2016, p23).

In teaching, rewarding students' achievements (behaviour) can impact on motivation and learning but only if used effectively. For instance, Black and Wiliam (1998, p24) note, *The use of extrinsic rewards can be counter-productive if they focus attention on 'ability' rather than on the belief that one's effort can produce success*. In support of this, Dweck (2017) argues that praising a student's ability can perpetuate their fixed mindset and lead to their reduced participation, for fear of exposure.

The further reading section at the end of this chapter will signpost you to much more information about behaviourism but for now we will move on to a reaction against it that, although appeared much earlier, can be seen to be growing significantly in the 1970s (Woollard, 2010).

Thinking about learning: moving beyond the lab rats

As a riposte to the behaviourist school, and building on the argument that it did not consider brain functioning, cognitivism quickly became a prominent concept for learning. Cognitivism is concerned with the process of thinking (cognition) and understanding, and cognitive functioning is how our brains deal with stimuli. What do we do with the bombardment of information we receive? How do we process it? Do we filter it first or merely store everything, with a view to using it later or forgetting it once it is agreed that it did not come in handy? How do we filter? How do we store? Surely, storage cannot be merely the images or sounds that come into our heads? The brain is where we understand stimuli and where we create meaning. Information is thus processed and converted into understanding. For instance, a picture of a cat, the letters 'c' 'a' and 't' combined, and an actual cat walking across the floor can all be observed and processed to have the same meaning.

In an attempt to address this, a number of theorists emerged. Piaget (1952), for instance, suggested that the process of understanding involves *schema*, *assimilation* and *accommodation*. An individual has a *schema* – a system of understanding in their heads – which produces knowledge. Schemata (plural of schema) have been analogised to index cards in the brain (Wadsworth, 2004), making meaning from incoming information (ideas and new experiences) by assimilating it into the appropriate schema. Schemata adapt, however, if the new information challenges our existing thinking, and this leads to *accommodation* where we form a new understanding. When we understand, we experience *equilibrium*. But if we are challenged, and do not understand something, we experience *disequilibrium*. According to the theory, we are motivated to learn in order to return to equilibrium.

To view this a different way, your brain is your filing cabinet of knowledge. If your friend hands you a document (information), you need to decide which file (schema) it goes in (assimilation). However, it may mean throwing out some of the old contents of the file because they are outdated or wrong (accommodation). Our filing cabinets are unique to us and this means that when we think of a concept – perhaps introduced in a lecture – we may think about it differently from our colleagues who also attended the same lecture. This individual cognitive process is our understanding. Facts are thus stored in a meaningful way that draw on personal experience. Consider this – someone mentions the following period: 1939–1945. Most of us will identify this as the period of the Second World War; however, those who lived through this period will probably have vastly different conceptualisations of it.

Cognitivism suggests that understanding is unique to the individual, and constructivism (where students 'construct' meaning) is sometimes seen as a subset of this, although many argue the distinction. In constructivism, individuals 'construct' understanding based on their experiences; therefore, knowledge is not merely internalised, it is actively built. Constructivism is *grounded in the research of Piaget, Bruner, Dewey, and Vygotsky* and is *increasingly influential today* (Woolfolk Hoy et al., 2013, p10).

Assessing understanding

In teaching, we attempt to measure knowledge and understanding through students' performance: usually through their demonstration or explanation. We believe that understanding occurs when a student's conceptualisation – as measured through assessment – coincides with ours. Thus, the student's schema for a particular piece of information resembles ours.

 Learning exercise

During a series of related calculations for a larger activity, one of your students has made a mistake. Try to identify the point at which they went wrong – that is, you need to compare your student's construction with yours. What pitfalls did they experience? Where did they go wrong? Try to put yourself in the student's shoes to understand their schema for this process. Can you identify the point where their construction (understanding) diverged from what you wanted? This is often easier to do with maths when it is systematic and is why your maths teacher at school always told you to 'show your working out'.

The spiral curriculum

As part of the cognitive process of learning, according to Vygotsky, Bruner and Ausubel (among others), students build on their existing understanding. Therefore, new learning cannot be meaningless and too abstract; it must connect to, and build on, information that the student already has. In this way, context is important and learning occurs when information is linked to a schema (assimilation). For example, *problems are frequently experienced when applying knowledge from a school subject to other subjects in contexts outside of school* (Illeris, 2009, p13). Building on existing meaning is effective and it allows us to feel reassurance.

This can be achieved through Bruner's (1960) concept of a spiral curriculum as it enables teachers to revisit areas – which are meaningful – and to develop them further each time; thus, knowledge is spiralling bigger and bigger. The concept of a spiral curriculum is significant because it connects with memory, and repetition can lead to embedment. A skill, for instance, is formed through practice (the old adage is right) and the repetition of this skill encourages the brain to develop new neuronal pathways in order to 'learn' the skill. Repetition merely tells your brain that it is important and thus needs its own pathway within the brain's network as it will be drawn on time and time again. Here's how you can combine the spiral curriculum in practice.

 **In practice**

You need to introduce a complex concept to your learners but they are not yet ready. Let's suppose you want to look at fractions and division. In order to know how to divide fractions, your students will need to master multiplication and, in particular, multiplying fractions, so these are covered in previous sessions; first, as number operations and then by applying multiplication to the fractions. Once you are at this stage, you can introduce division.

In the example below, the numerator (integer on the top) and denominator (integer on the bottom) of the second fraction are swapped around to invert it. This then becomes a simple multiplication. The numerators are multiplied against each other and then the same is done to the denominators:

$$\frac{3}{4} \div \frac{1}{4} \text{ becomes } \frac{3}{4} \times \frac{4}{1} = \frac{12}{4} \text{ or 3 (simplified)}$$

This example has been deliberately chosen because it illustrates the process clearly. It can be worked out by merely looking at it: how many quarters are there in three quarters? The fraction is then simplified because it is 'top-heavy'. Twelve quarters? Well, every four quarters is a whole one so this must be three whole ones. If you are still unsure of what has happened, cut up three pieces of A4 paper into four parts each. Each part is a quarter and you have twelve altogether. How many whole ones can you make by reassembling them (imagine somebody else cut them up)? You can reproduce this exercise with your students if they are struggling.

 **In practice**

The spiral curriculum can be more comprehensive than this, of course. Supposing your students absolutely detest fractions (it does happen) and need a sensitive approach to help them eliminate the many barriers they have acquired over the years. Even the simple addition of one-half and one-quarter is enough to generate anxiety. A few weeks before they reach fractions, incorporate some of the terminology of fractions into the discourse but do not make too much of it. In a discussion on safeguarding, for instance, you may disclose some statistics about domestic violence, a concern for approximately 27 per cent of women and 13 per cent of men (**www.ons.gov.uk/**). If you suggest this is around one in three women and approximately one in four men, you have two fractions you can introduce. Let's assume that your learners will more than likely be familiar with these. (If they are not, you will have to address this beforehand.) You can then point out to them that they can demonstrate the equivalence between a fraction and its percentage.

More subtly, put the one in three on the board as a fraction but do not place too much emphasis on fractions; rather, return to them a little later. The point of this is to lay a foundation in order to build on it at a later date (or later in the session if they are ready). You may find that the next statistics you draw on relate to one-third of people categorised in one way and one-third categorised in another. How many is that all together, you ask? If you get the required response then you can illustrate this in the following fashion:

Yes, that's right. A third and a third is two thirds. $\frac{1}{3} + \frac{1}{3} = \frac{2}{3}$

Again, you may choose to not even mention the F word, instead relying on a little inculcation. If you can, develop this in the session: point out how you got that answer outside of drawing it from memory. Aim to get your students thinking about what it looks like on paper – what Bruner calls the iconic, which we shall explore below. If they ask questions, develop it, take it further but try to avoid overdoing it because you don't want to feed their barriers. Use a cake or a pizza or whatever you think is a useful teaching aid but try to find something your students will relate to. Then make a judgement call. If they have had enough, do something different. The purpose of this is not to cover fractions now, but to give the students many tasters over a number of weeks to reduce anxiety for when the time comes.

Each time you do this, you are building on what you have done previously and if done over time you should be able to get around many of your students' barriers towards fractions. This also allows you to build in complexity as you introduce difficult concepts over time. When you return to the subject, there will be some familiarity and the students should become more relaxed as time goes on. Not only are you familiarising your students with a tricky area, you are developing their knowledge along the way. That is, the level of complexity can increase because they are ready for it.

Getting your students in the zone

Lev Vygotsky claimed that learning was social (compare this with the work of Lave and Wenger (2009)) and that there is a zone that, for maximum effect, a student needs to be in when working. This is called the zone of proximal development (Vygotsky, 1978) and it works as shown in Figure 3.1.

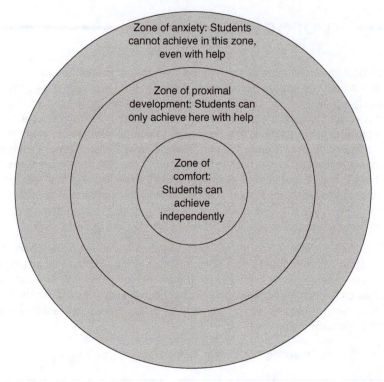

Figure 3.1 Zone of proximal development

In the diagram, there are three zones to exemplify the process. The zone of comfort (ZC) is one in which the students can easily achieve something. This is what they could do even if you had not turned up that day. In the zone of anxiety, achievement is not possible, at least not until they have worked through the zone of proximal development (ZPD). The ZPD, then, is the focus and the one where your facilitation counts as it requires a more-knowledgeable other (MKO) to work with the students. In this zone, the students need your support and can do more with this support than by working alone (without your support they remain in the ZC). To get your students out of their comfort zones, you will need to set a task that challenges them. Your task must be one that they can work on but also one that you will be required to facilitate the progress of; that is, have an input, make suggestions, and provide guidance. Steer them, then, towards completing the task but do not provide too much guidance as this can reduce the complexity and push them back into their ZC.

The zone of anxiety (ZA) is where understanding or ability is not yet where it needs to be. Have you set something that is too hard and cannot be achieved, even with your help? Perhaps you are jumping too high, too soon – remember the spiral curriculum. If so, the help the students need may be too much, whereupon *you* are completing the task instead of them. However, once your students do complete a task, you will need to raise the complexity for their next challenge. In this way, an activity that was previously in the zone of anxiety may move to the ZPD.

You may decide that the students can return to their ZC occasionally. Learning isn't always about moving forward with new information, and processing what we know and undergoing reflection can often help with consolidation and raise our self-esteem. Of course, once the students have mastered the skill(s) they are working on, or have seemingly acquired the necessary knowledge, they will need to move on, and this is a judgement call that will become easier as you get to know them.

The importance of the ZPD in today's teaching relates to stretch and challenge. Thus, we should ask more from our students than they can do alone. In this way, they are stretched, they learn more effectively, and we do what we love – teach.

Representing meaning

For understanding, Bruner (1960) identifies three modes of representation:

1. symbolic;

2. iconic;

3. enactive.

In *art and design*, your students are expected to understand the artistic features of a key construction. To understand on a symbolic level, you merely have to say the descriptor for each building and your students know what you are referring to. This is meaningful and this level is the goal for learning. To illustrate this, we can look at the Eiffel Tower. Supposing a student does not know what you mean when you use this term. You can revert to level 2 in the list (iconic) and show them a picture. That's still no good, as it does not mean anything. OK, so let's move to the enactive. You organise a visit to Paris and show your students the Eiffel Tower (and hopefully they can sketch/paint it whilst they are there). In future, when you show them the picture again, they should make the connection; thus, you have represented the Eiffel Tower iconically. If they understand further, and can evidence language skills (particularly those that many of us take for granted), then you can represent the Eiffel Tower symbolically by merely using its name. This is an extreme, and largely simplistic, example (involving much expense as you trek across Europe just to see the Parisian delights) but you hopefully get the picture (pun intended).

 In practice

Using money (can apply in most subjects). Supposing the phrase three times seven did not mean anything to one of your students. Moreover, a pictorial representation of three lots of seven coins is equally meaningless. Your next step is to move to the enactive. You lay out 21 coins in three piles and your student now has something more concrete to work with. Your goal, then, is to reach the symbolic.

While the example is merely a basic illustration of the concept, the complexity can easily be added. It's not rocket science! But it could be: atmospheric pressure is difficult to represent symbolically but may be needed on your *Basic Guide to Astronautical Engineering* course. Fortunately, demonstrations with sealed containers can help for reification. Thus, the enactive is often useful to go back to and using these modes of representation as loose guides might help you to diagnose the difficulty level of something you are teaching. Are you pitching it too high? Alternatively, are you failing to stretch your learners by showing them what they already know and can demonstrate?

Humanism

Like behaviourism, the cognitive school of how we learn is, for humanists, inadequate as it is fixated with interpretation (meaning) and understanding (meaning-making), rather than focused on individuals and their personal goals and motivations. Although it has its roots in the early twentieth century with figures such as Montessori, humanism became popular in the 1960s and 1970s as it proved to be a worthy opponent of behaviourism and cognitivism (Bates, 2016). Its premise lies with free will, self-development and personal empowerment, and teaching is advocated as a learner-centred activity. As such, it ties in with the individual meaning-making aspect of constructivism.

Humanism is very much in existence in today's educational thinking and can be seen in many strategies, such as *discovery learning* and *experiential learning* (elements of which stem from the early work of John Dewey), the *flipped classroom* – a strategy where your input can be given to the students beforehand (in the form of a video) so that the session is devoted to activities and the focus is on the students – and *individual learning plans* that account for, and record, personal growth. Due to its concentration on the individual, therefore, it is fuelled by intrinsic motivation.

Key figures in humanistic teaching include Maslow (1908–1970), Rogers (1902–1987) and Knowles (1913–1997).

Maslow's hierarchy of needs, although having been criticised much, suggests that humans have basic needs (from breathing and eating to self-fulfilment) and each must be met before the students can move to the next level. The end goal is self-actualisation and ties in with the work of Carl Rogers in that it is personal growth towards the self we want to be. The five needs can be seen below, with number one being the most basic:

1. physiological;

2. safety;

3. belonging;

4. esteem;

5. self-actualisation.

Rogers believed in teachers as facilitators, rather than as experts, whose role it is to draw on the experiences of adults to help them to learn in a personally meaningful way. Teaching, then, is more about providing the right environment and then guiding the students towards an appropriate goal (Bates, 2016).

Knowles differentiates between adults' and children's learning, suggesting that *pedagogy* is related to teaching children and is about imparting information, whereas what he terms *andragogy* involves the teaching of adults and is learner-centred, drawing on the life experiences of the students. Thus, meaning must fit into their existing understandings and experiences which have been individually shaped by their interactions with the world. Compare this with Ausubel's (1968) deductive reasoning and meaningful learning, whereby a person will learn by building on what they already know.

 **In practice**

How can I use humanism in my teaching?

In the humanist approach, learners have individual needs and the process of differentiation can be seen explicitly in many functional skills classes, where identified ability can range from entry level 2 to level 2. Thus, goals are individual and the use of a personal learning plan can help to identify these. In developing this, students work through personal goals and thus progress at different rates.

The humanist approach calls for learner-centred activities and collaborative work may need to be worked out in advance in order to strategise the mix of abilities. For instance, what experiences do the students bring to the group? Is the group working on the same area and at the same level? Or, are they working at different levels whereby you can incorporate Vygotsky's ZPD for peer learning – a learner who has already achieved a skill can act as the MKO to support another who is working towards it.

Resources may need to be varied in order to take into account ability. For example, some may be able to represent information using Bruner's symbolic, whilst others may be at the enactive level. One criticism of this approach is that when planning for a large number of students in a single session, you could potentially be preparing several lessons at once.

Sociocultural approaches and situated learning

Central to sociocultural learning is the cultural context in which social relationships are enacted (Woolfolk Hoy *et al.*, 2013). This perspective on learning is particularly valid today as diversity, inclusion and multicultural perspectives are a significant feature in our society. Learning is thus viewed as a process drawn from our interactions with the world, and through our involvement with others. For teaching, social practices and cultural perspectives are intertwined and effective education will sit within this process.

Students, particularly adults, will exhibit many sociocultural barriers, such as misconceptions of gender (believing that the maths world is masculine and more suited to men, while English is a feminine pursuit, particularly where literature plays a role), peer pressure, family beliefs impinging on expectations, and social deprivation – particularly where priorities lie elsewhere – along with many other factors that, at the very least, are a major distraction for students.

A common argument throughout this book is that learning needs to be meaningful and the socio-cultural approach can support this. Maths and English are often deemed to be irrelevant in life but this misconception is usually based on perceiving maths as algebra, calculus, trigonometry and so on, and English as Shakespeare, Dickens and the like. When connections are made between decimals and money, percentages and shopping, or between grammar and writing a letter for a job, or spelling and the compiling of a CV, maths and English may be perceived with much relevance. Understanding the sociocultural factors of your group will help you to determine potential barriers and to tailor your teaching to meet their needs, expectations, and even wishes.

Moreover, it has been argued that students learn when they are 'situated' in the learning experience – such as an apprentice plumber engaged on a building site – and that they move from *legitimate peripheral participation* (as a newcomer) to *full participation* (as a qualified professional) in a *community of practice* (Lave and Wenger, 2009). Learning occurs, then, through social participation, rather than as an individual act of knowledge acquisition. As such, it is *an evolving, continuously renewed set of relations* (Lave and Wenger, 2009, p50). However, learning is arguably meaningful; it is related to the job/career and often ties in with the learner's motivation (whether intrinsic or extrinsic).

Embedding maths and English works well when it functions in this way. The apprentice plumber knows that they have to measure, conduct a calculation on, and bend, a pipe to install a fully working sink in a real-life kitchen. For them, maths is both relevant and necessary. Therefore, a consideration of the community of practice that your learners are looking to interact with may help you to tailor your teaching to incorporate greater meaning for them.

 ── Learning exercise ──

Think about your classroom in a typical teaching session. Do you feel that the students are part of a community of practice? Is there anybody that you could identify as being more on the periphery than at the centre? What strategies can you employ to change this?

Learning domains

Bloom's Taxonomy (Bloom *et al.*, 1956) is well known throughout the education world for its identification of three domains of learning: the *cognitive*, the *psychomotor* and the *affective*. The popularity of this concept is perhaps its ability to straddle the various approaches of mind, body and emotion. That is, it acknowledges cognitive and behavioural functioning and identifies emotional connection (which includes attitude). From a teaching perspective, the domains encourage teachers to consider the various aspects involved in learning. In the cognitive domain, there are various categories – the original ones were *Knowledge, Comprehension, Application, Analysis, Synthesis* and *Evaluation*, although these have since been revised (see Krathwohl, 2002) – that facilitate the development of complexity so that teachers can differentiate and build in levels of difficulty.

In practice

In your maths-embedded session, you have decided to teach ratio in construction. Through your earlier use of the spiral curriculum, you have encouraged your students to adopt a different attitude towards maths (affective). You are now going to draw on the cognitive and psychomotor domains for the next step. Three groups of students are designing an outbuilding but each one has different requirements and therefore requires more bricks. Design one requires 289 bricks, design two has three times more than this, and design three has two times more than the second one. The ratio, then, is 1:3:6. How many bricks are needed in total? If orders are per thousand, how many orders will be needed?

You can also raise the complexity of this by changing the ratio to include decimals (3.25 times bigger, for instance) and as a project you can build in many more elements of the construction such as calculating the cost for each design, generating an average cost, and then building in English skills by asking them to write an advert to promote the sale of each design. For psychomotor, you can use small, plastic blocks/bricks to represent the real bricks and ask your students to divide them up accordingly. For example, 100 plastic bricks becomes 10 for design one, 30 for design two, and 60 for design three.

Learning exercise

In your reading, find information and takes notes on *Structure of Observed Learning Outcome* (SOLO) Taxonomy. How does this compare to Bloom's Taxonomy?

Mindsets

Carol Dweck's concept of *growth mindset* (GM) is rapidly infiltrating schools throughout Britain as well as many other countries. The strength of this is the theoretical underpinning and robust research that has fuelled the argument. Dweck is respected in the academic community and although the concept is not exactly new, her development of it is admirable. Moreover, it is widely accessible to schools, unlike, unfortunately, some 'blue skies' research that can sit in top academic journals (albeit the landscape is changing with the introduction of impact as part of universities' research funding and Open Access journals).

A fixed mindset is viewed as limiting; it is one where an individual believes that intelligence (often measured through IQ tests) and skills are fixed traits and therefore ability is constrained by this. This would suggest that there are some things in life that you just cannot do unless you have a natural flair for them. Those with a fixed mindset believe in talent over hard work. Dweck's research challenges this view and limitations (with the exception of learning difficulties and/or disabilities) are generally only self-imposed. Many students feel they are either good at maths or good at English, but not both, whereby their perceived ability can act as a barrier, even if this is high. If ability is perceived to be natural, and the view that people are either talented or not is taken, then hard work and effort may not be applied. So, when someone illustrates great ability, they may be labelled as being a natural. This is a nice position to be in, you might think, but when combined with a fixed mindset it results in a fear of failure.

In her book, Dweck (2017) relates stories of athletes who were at the top of their game but when things did not go as they were supposed to for a *natural*, they avoided performing for fear of losing the title. They bought into the thinking that success was innate and not related to effort, causing those other athletes who did persevere with effort to overtake them. The apparently not-so-gifted worked harder when they had a growth mindset and this led to them becoming winners. Success, then, is seen to be representative of attitude and the make-or-break aspect of performing is thus dependent on the mind.

One of the key ingredients of GM is the comment to students that they 'are not there yet'. In this way, students are encouraged to believe in themselves and to keep working towards their goals. Ability is not fixed, but rather dependent on experience and hard work. In the words of the great Sophocles himself, *Nothing succeeds without toil.*

As a teacher, you can encourage your students to adopt a GM and such an outlook can increase motivation and achievement; hopefully, this will result in greater resilience against failure and a love of learning. The story of Edison (with the help of a generally unacknowledged team of scientists) having discovered the lightbulb for the 2,000th time may be exaggerated or even a myth, but it serves as a good example of perseverance (Bates, 2016). His claim is that he discovered 1,999 ways that the light would not work, rather than having failed this number of times. Moral: if you get knocked down, get up, dust yourself off, and try again.

 Learning exercise

Can you identify those among your students with fixed mindsets and those with growth mindsets? How do their approaches to activities vary? Note three differences that you can use in your teaching.

Action research

Perhaps as a result of the variability of human nature when theory is applied to practice, action research has become popular in recent years. Action research can enable personal growth and can help teachers to target areas that are specific to them or to their school. In this way, research becomes less generic and personalised and it is this particular aspect that can be attractive to teachers. When presented with research findings, an arguably common response from teachers is, 'How can I use this?' Many teachers would like to attend a conference or research seminar, learn of a strategy, and then use this in their teaching the next day – and understandably so. However, research mostly does not work in this way and only usually contributes small steps towards our overall knowledge of teaching and learning. This is frustrating, particularly for busy schools and colleges that are under much performative pressure to achieve and to satisfy policy requirements. Action research, therefore, has much appeal as it can bring the results that are relevant to *your* practice. A typical action research project can be seen in the following example.

In practice

A teacher has a problem, identifies the concern, plans a strategy for resolving the problem (takes action), reviews the concern, and evaluates the approach through reflection. If necessary, the teacher tries again with a revised strategy. The process is cyclical. Here's what it could look like in practice:

You want to explore the impact of group work when approaching a problem. You split the class into several groups and give each one a different methodology. Everyone in group one is equal and therefore must decide amongst themselves how to approach the problem. In group two, you allocate a role for each member, to vary the contributions: Project Leader, Timekeeper, Labourer and so on. Group three is divided into two subgroups and each one has a widely different approach to the problem; therefore, the subgroup with the best argument (refereed by a neutral person) will lead. Observe the impact of the relationships in each group and identify a suitable assessment process to measure each one. You may have decided to use a fourth group as assessors. What worked? What needed changing? Reflect on the process, evaluate it, and perhaps try the exercise with another class, acknowledging the potential variables of each, of course.

Context: author's perspective

Learning that is meaningful can be more effective than committing something arbitrary to mind, such as a PIN code (Illeris, 2009); therefore, context is extremely important. Without it, there may be numerous barriers that need addressing. From my own experience, I recall a particular maths session when I was around 15 years old. I was called upon to calculate the circumference of a circle and I remember feeling that I had missed a lesson, despite the fact that my attendance was 100 per cent. I was told to multiply the diameter by 3.142.

Why?

Because that's pi.

Pie? What's that? What are you talking about?

My mind flitted to pies and pizzas and other aspects of maths teaching that are used to explain fractions and I never made the connection for some time. Nobody explained to me what pi was. I merely accepted it, perceived that my maths ability was inadequate and that I obviously did not understand a substantial amount of mathematical concepts, and carried on to do as well as I could, given the circumstances.

It was not until some years later that I understood the use of pi in such calculations, by which time it was my own learning maverick self that needed to know. But many learners are not this motivated (or nerdy!). Even now, many years later, this experience is vivid in my mind and the confusion I had throughout this period from this and other examples of bad teaching was extremely problematic. For years, I struggled with circumference (and maths in general). I enjoyed writing and fell into the fixed-mindset trap of thinking that maths was not for me. Even at times when I felt that I understood the rule it would slip out my head, forced aside by the memories of poor learning (or poor teaching?). The situation could have been so different, if only my teacher had said something along the lines of the following:

This is a calculation that has already been worked out by some clever mathematicians in ancient civilizations. For every circle, regardless of its size, we can calculate the circumference by multiplying the diameter with this measurement. The measurement is a mathematical constant and works every time. All you need to do is remember its (approximate) value.

Up until this point I enjoyed maths. This example, therefore, illustrates that even something seemingly insignificant can impact on your learners' motivation and self-belief.

 ── Learning exercise ──

Thinking about your own experiences, have there been occasions when you didn't understand something in a lesson but felt obliged to move on, perhaps through a fear of being labelled as stupid? This is how some of your learners may feel.

 ── Chapter summary ──

Theory is a useful tool for supporting teaching and context provides for a more meaningful experience that can concretize the learning experience. If it's relevant for the students, it's likely to be more memorable for them because they feel they will need to draw on it again.

This chapter has explored:

- What do we know?
- Why use theory?
- Whistle-stop tour of behaviourism.
- Early behaviourism.
- Modern behaviourism.
- Thinking about learning: moving beyond the lab rats.
- Assessing understanding.
- The spiral curriculum.
- Getting your students in the zone.
- Representing meaning.
- Humanism.
- How can I use humanism in my teaching?

- Sociocultural approaches and situated learning.
- Learning domains.
- Mindsets.
- Action research.
- Context: author's perspective.

Further reading

Aubrey, K and Riley, A (2015) *Understanding and Using Educational Theories*. London: Sage.

Illeris, K (ed) *Contemporary Theories of Learning: Learning Theorists ... In Their Own Words*. New York: Taylor & Francis.

Palmer, J, Bresler, L and Cooper, DE (eds) (2001) *Fifty Major Thinkers on Education: From Confucius to Dewey*. New York: Taylor & Francis.

Palmer, J, Bresler, L and Cooper, DE (eds) (2001) *Fifty Modern Thinkers on Education: From Piaget to the Present*. New York: Taylor & Francis.

Phillips, DC and Soltis, JF (2009) *Perspectives on Learning*. 5th edn. New York: Teachers College Press.

References

Ausubel, DP (1968) *Educational Psychology: A Cognitive View*. New York: Holt, Rinehart and Winston Inc.

Bates, B (2016) *Learning Theories Simplified ... And How to Apply Them to Teaching*. London: Sage.

Black, P and Wiliam, D (1998) Assessment and classroom learning, *Assessment in Education: Principles, Policy & Practice*, 5(1): 7–74.

Bloom, BS (ed) Engelhart, MD, Furst, EJ, Hill, WH and Krathwohl, DR (1956) *Taxonomy of Educational Objectives, Handbook I: The Cognitive Domain*. New York: David McKay Co Inc.

Bruner, J (1960) *The Process of Education*. Cambridge, Massachusetts: Harvard University Press.

Dweck, C (2017) *Mindset: Changing the Way You Think to Fulfil Your Potential*. London: Robinson.

Illeris, K (2009) A comprehensive understanding of human learning, in Illeris, K (ed) *Contemporary Theories of Learning: Learning Theorists ... In Their Own Words*. New York: Taylor & Francis.

Krathwohl, DR (2002) A revision of Bloom's Taxonomy: an overview, *Theory into Practice*, 41(4): 212–18.

Lave, J and Wenger, E (2009) *Situated Learning: Legitimate Peripheral Participation*. Cambridge: Cambridge University Press.

Olson, MH and Hergenhahn, BR (2016) *Introduction to Theories of Learning*. 9th edn. London: Routledge.

Petty, G (2014) *Teaching Today: A Practical Guide.* 5th edn. Oxford: Oxford University Press.

Piaget, J (1952) *The Origins of Intelligence in Children.* New York: International Universities Press.

Vygotsky, L (1978) *Mind in Society.* Cambridge, Massachusetts: Harvard University Press.

Wadsworth, BJ (2004) *Piaget's Theory of Cognitive and Affective Development: Foundations of Constructivism.* London: Longman Publishing.

Woolfolk Hoy, A, Davis, HA and Anderman, EM (2013) Theories of learning and teaching in *TIP'*, *Theory into Practice*, 52(1): 9–21.

Woollard, J (2010) *Psychology for the Classroom: Behaviourism.* New York: Taylor & Francis.

▬ Useful websites ▬

Learning theories

- **www.learning-theories.com/**

- **www.education.com/reference/article/theories-of-learning/**

- **http://infed.org/mobi/learning-theory-models-product-and-process/**

- **http://teachinglearningresources.pbworks.com/**

Mindset – **www.mindsetworks.com/science/**

NEA (document) – **http://files.eric.ed.gov/fulltext/ED495823.pdf**

Psychology

- **http://infed.org/mobi/learning-theory-models-product-and-process/**

- **http://m.simplypsychology.org/bandura.html**

4
Strategies for embedding maths

 This chapter

In this chapter, strategies for incorporating maths into different subject areas, particularly vocational, are explored. Maths skills can be embedded into most subjects and the level of complexity can vary, resulting in much scope for differentiating activities. The chosen maths skills for this chapter mirror the current functional skills criteria at various levels as the *functional* aspect of these is particularly relevant. The purpose of this is also to identify the level that is required for those particular skills. Thus, although functional skills are undergoing major revision, this is seen to be irrelevant as the focus here is on embedding various maths skills and understanding the different levels. The criteria, then, merely act as a useful guide for nationally agreed skill equivalences.

This chapter will cover:

- Embedding naturally.
- Mixed abilities.
- Maths in practice.
- Raising the complexity.

Embedding naturally

Embedding maths and English in your teaching may seem daunting but it is often just a matter of thinking outside the box, as they say. For instance, even when arranging your class into group activities you can introduce simplistic strategies. Consider the following scenario:

Teacher: I need you all to work in groups of two for this activity. How many of us are there? [Teacher does a quick head count] Seventeen, that means we can have … Rachel, you're good at maths. How many twos go into 17?

Rachel: Nine [thinks]. No, eight. Eight twos is …

Teacher: Or, two eights?

Rachel: Two eights …16. Eight groups and one left over.

Teacher: Good. One of the groups can work in a three.

Later on, the groups are asked to feed back to the main class on what they have learned from the activity.

Teacher: We'll start with this group and then we'll move in an anti-clockwise direction. If this group is first [selecting a group near the centre] then which group would be next?

Floella: Our group.

Teacher: Yes. Well done, Floella. Then the next group …?

This may seem very basic but there are two important points here. First, you are not saying to your students that you are teaching them maths; the situation is almost naturally occurring. Second, what is the level of the students? What are their English and maths capabilities? Some students will not know how to tell the time. Some will have difficulty with division. Some will struggle with communication, or they may have very little self-esteem and this needs to be managed sensitively. There are many aspects of English and maths covered, even in this brief description, and with experience you will be able to incorporate many more. Moreover, what employability skills have they developed? Teamwork? Team leading? Communication and interpersonal skills? Decision-making? Many of these really are part and parcel of what we teach every day.

Table 4.1 Ofqual recognises the following equivalences

Level	Equivalent
L3	A/AS Level
L2	GCSE (grades A*-C)
L1	GCSE (grades D-G)
E3	Pre-GCSE

(Source: **www.accreditedqualifications.org.uk/**)

Mixed abilities

Although you will be mostly dealing with students of level 1 and 2 ability (colleges often require this information from students in order for them to enrol), you may have learners at entry level (see Table 4.1), such as those with a learning difficulty or disability, so you will need to tailor your activities accordingly. Moreover, some institutions, such as private training providers or alternative learning programmes, will be supporting students who have missed much of their compulsory English and maths education yet excel practically. This has previously caused concern and the strategy of foundation learning – although no longer applicable – aimed to address it, allowing students to have a spiky profile; for example, they could be working towards entry 2 in maths yet towards level 1 in bricklaying. However, this is problematic because progression is often limited until the students' English and/or maths ability reaches the same level as their practical ability.

Although this book explores a number of strategies, it is not a 'how to teach maths' text; rather, it is focused on the strategic embedding of mathematical (and English) ability within your specific subject. As such, the details for the calculations may occasionally be left out and the remit of this book does not allow for various ways of approaching a problem to be explored. For instance, long division was long taught using the 'bus stop' method but is now often taught using 'chunking', drawing on multiplication to arrive at the answer. Such techniques can be found in most maths books and are therefore omitted.

 Learning exercise

Investigate your institution's strategy for supporting maths and English study and identify what contribution you can make.

Maths in practice

Add and subtract using three-digit numbers (E3/L1)

 Scenario

In fashion and retail, a customer purchases the following three items: a dress (priced at £142), a pair of shoes (£101) and a coat (£225). The till has unfortunately broken, just this morning, and you are required to add up the total cost of the items. You don't have a calculator to hand and your phone is in the staff room because of the shop rules. As your customer is becoming irate, you will need to use what is at your disposal - a pen and some paper.

The student can work through the calculation once you have illustrated your preferred method. For example, you may ask them to lay out the figures in this way:

$$142$$

$$101$$

$$+\ \underline{225}$$

Starting on the right, the students can work through each column by adding the digit on each row. This will involve 'carrying' numbers and if there are problems with counting then beads can be used. This is not the only method of doing this, of course, but the important aspect here is that you are relating the mathematical calculation to the chosen subject, and thus your preferred method of approaching this can be substituted.

The next stage would be for the customer to change her mind and decide to leave one of the items, requiring the student to subtract the value of that item. One aspect to note is the use of a zero, which can complicate matters and thus raise the level needed to perform the calculation. When subtracting, for instance, the zero would need to be changed by borrowing. Again, there are many more modern ways to perform these calculations which you can explore. The level of complexity can be varied, depending on your students, and you can introduce pence as well as pound. This will also help you to cover, **Add and subtract decimals up to two decimal places (L1)** and **Carry out calculations with numbers of any size in practical contexts, to a given number of decimal places (L2)**.

Solve practical problems involving multiplication and division ... using a range of strategies (E3/L1)

Continuing with the above example, the customer wishes to purchase more than one of the same item. Perhaps she is also purchasing matching outfits for her seven grandchildren (priced at £11 each). We then need to multiply the outfit price by seven, and so on. After your student has calculated a price for the outfits, tell them that there is £2 off each one when purchases of five or more are made so that they can apply the relevant *division*. This question is layered and can apply to other levels by raising the complexity, which we shall explore a little later on.

Round to the nearest 10 or 100. Your students arrive at £63 for the outfits ($7 \times 11 = 77$ then $7 \times 2 = 14$ then $77 - 14 = \mathbf{63}$). What is this rounded off to the nearest 10, to the nearest 100? Does the figure go up or down? What is the rule for rounding off?

 In practice

Using Vygoysky's ZPD, you act as the more-knowledgeable other to scaffold the learning. Push your students and keep raising the complexity as they achieve, at the same time providing enough guidance to steer them in the right direction.

Understand and use simple fractions (E3). Understand and use equivalences between common fractions, decimals and percentages (L1/L2). Use simple formulae expressed in words for one- or two-step operations (L1). Understand and use simple formulae and equations involving one- or two-step operations (L2). Understand and use equivalences between common fractions, decimals and percentages (L1)

The following examples incorporate numerous criteria and you should aim to adopt this thinking throughout your teaching to make meaningful connections and to illustrate the relevance, and importance, of maths for the course as a whole.

Catering and hospitality

In small groups in one of your teaching sessions, the students bake a cake for the whole group (18 people). What fraction of cake does each person receive? If someone is absent and someone else has two pieces, what fraction do they have? Has this been simplified? What relationship can you identify between the 1/18 and the 2/18? Do your level 1s mistakenly identify this as 50 per cent bigger?

In your film studies teaching, the director's cut is one-third longer than the original. At entry level, choose a straightforward running time to ensure that the calculation can be performed – 3 hours for the original – and raise the bar for students functioning at higher levels – 1 hour and 28 minutes. What is 0.75 of the original running time? Can your students equate this to three-quarters or 75 per cent? Alfred Hitchcock is reputed to have said, *The* length of a film *should be directly related to the endurance of the human bladder* (Rose, 1995). Can you think of a mathematical formula for estimating this? Perhaps you can make one up for fun? Here's an attempt:

For anyone up to the age of 40:

Age of individual × 30 + 30 = average bladder capacity in ml. Then divide by 10 to give a running time in minutes before a break is needed.

So, for an 18-year-old:

$$18 \times 30 + 30/10 = 57$$

Thus, their capacity to sit through a film before they need a break would be 57 minutes (too many fizzy drinks!).

For anyone over the age of 40, you would divide by 15 instead of 10.

So, a 51-year-old could wait 1 hour and 44 minutes:

$$51 \times 30 + 30/15 = 104$$

Obviously, there are variables to consider: when did that person last visit the toilet? How much have they had to drink, and so on? So, this is merely a bit of fun but an arguably interesting way to practise using formulae. However, don't forget to stress to your students that this formula is *not* based on scientific evidence.

Back to your 3-hour film, then. How many breaks would you need to factor in for a 33-year-old male watching with his 29-year-old wife? This question develops as we now need to identify an average (mean) (***Find mean and range (L1)***). For this, we add the ages together (29 + 33) and then divide by two (because there are two numbers – one for each person) and we have our average: 31. Perhaps you have a family to account for and you want to calculate the breaks needed for your film. You have the following ages: 33, 29, 11 and 6. What is your average? Is there anything significant about this combination of numbers? You will notice that they range widely. (The range is calculated by taking away the lowest (6) from the highest (33).) This will result in an average that is maybe unsuitable for all, despite the fact that it is deemed to be 'average'. Your average age is now 20 (19.75) but that is too young for your adults and comparatively old for your children. The outliers, then, are contributing to your standard deviation (the range in age means that your average is not going to be an accurate reflection) and you could mention this if your students are pushing way beyond level 2. Furthermore, if one or two of the adults is over 40, your students will have to identify that a different formula is needed.

 Learning exercise

Once you are confident with embedding maths up to level 2, you may wish to consider exploring statistics and probability further to develop your professional ability. This will certainly help you when teaching at level 2. Could you eventually teach the standard of A level, however? (Warning! Maths can be addictive.)

Understand, estimate, measure and compare length, capacity, weight and temperature (E3–L2)

Sport science NVQ

What is the volume of the swimming pool? How do we calculate this? What temperature does the water need to be? What temperature is it now? Can we calculate the surface area of the water first? (This might involve reading from a chart for pre-level 1 but you should encourage students to attempt formulae where appropriate.)

What is the target weight for the adult male you have identified in a table? By how much is he overweight? Perhaps you bring in some everyday items for realism and some specialist sports equipment then ask your students to estimate the weight. How far off were they? Do they have a fair gauge of weight or are they way off? Can you link this with fractions or percentages if the measurement is appropriate? For instance, your students estimated that one piece of equipment weighed 10kg yet it weighed 15kg. What is the percentage/fractional difference? The actual weight is 150 per cent, or one and a half times, heavier. Do your students understand why 50 per cent is 5 and not 7.5? In other words, have they calculated 50 per cent of the actual weight instead?

 ── In practice ──

In Ausubel's (1968) theory of meaningful knowledge, individuals build on existing understanding. In the examples throughout this chapter, think about whether you are building on prior learning. Is what you are doing meaningful for your students or irrelevant? That is, can they relate to it?

Understand decimals to two decimal places in practical contexts (E3). Convert units of measure in the same system (L1)

The key phrase here is 'practical contexts', as this applies to all the criteria. The content needs to be 'functional' and relevant, and fit in with the subject area. Where possible, it is particularly engaging if it fits into your students' social experiences too.

> *Where the subject under study is solely maths or English, such as standalone functional skills qualifications, it may be easier to link the content to your learners' lives as there is more flexibility to tailor the questions, i.e. they are not factoring in a vocational area.*

Textiles

Your students have converted the measurement of set pieces of cloth from imperial to metric (***Use, convert and calculate using metric and, where appropriate, imperial measures (L2)***) and are faced with large numbers. Can they round them off to two decimal places? Do they know the value of each digit? Place value charts are useful ways of helping students to categorise numbers and thus to understand value.

Illustrate how the figures can be multiplied and where in the place value table they would move to. Also, you can bring in ratio and proportion and scale to this exercise for your higher-level learn-ers (***Solve simple problems involving ratio, where one number is a multiple of the other (L1). Understand, use and calculate ratio and proportion, including problems involving scale (L2)***). For instance, this piece of cloth is a scaled representative as you need a larger piece for a mainstream exhibition. The scale is 1:100, so 1cm of material = 100cm (or 1m) in reality. You can ask them to multiply the value by 100 to record the actual size of the material needed. However, you can elevate the complexity to further incorporate differentiation and ask them to measure the material in mm. So, your measurement is 388mm and that equates to 38.8 which they multiply by 100. Or, they multiply the original by 1,000 if they are confident with conversions. (This is not an abstract exercise so if you are finding this difficult to envisage, use actual measurements, a ruler and so on, and even materials, to see how it works in practice.)

Your final figure gives them an indication of what two decimal places looks like and as an introduc-tion this could provide a baseline for when you work with larger numbers, particularly where the students have to reduce the overall figure to two decimal places. Thus, the process is cyclical but you may wish to take extracts from this, rather than attempting every step in a single session.

Using a generic example. In a workplace, there is a mixture of 64 men and 192 women. What is the proportion of women to men; what is the ratio? The total number is 256. So for proportion,

$$\text{Women} = \frac{192}{256} \text{ (which simplifies to } \frac{3}{4}\text{)}$$

$$\text{Men} = \frac{64}{256} \text{ (which simplifies to } \frac{1}{4}\text{)}$$

For ratio, we know that the figures represent quarters of the total so let's divide 256 by 4. This gives us 64 as one-quarter. We then divide 192 by 64 (= 3) and 64 by 64 (= 1) to give us a ratio of 3:1.

There are three times more women in this workplace than men. If you are not sure how to simplify (or have simply forgotten), you would do well to have a refresher or consult a source such as a textbook. YouTube is often good for finding a video that will explain things clearly. For now, however, here is a very quick overview:

$\frac{64}{256}$ can be broken down because both integers are divisible by at least one number other than one (dividing by one merely takes you back to where you started). There are many answers, so if in doubt try the usual suspects: 2, 3, 5, etc. Dividing by two will take a bit longer as the larger the number you divide by the quicker it will be but it is often easier. Dividing by two (halving) will look like this:

$$\frac{64}{256} \qquad \frac{32}{128} \qquad \frac{16}{64} \qquad \frac{8}{32} \qquad \frac{4}{16} \qquad \frac{2}{8} \qquad \frac{1}{4}$$

The trick is to keep going until saturation (it can no longer be reduced). Alternatively, if you see that 256 is divisible by 64, you could jump straight to 1 and 4:

$$\frac{1}{4}$$

Some students will need to divide by two and some may see the 64. As such, the emphasis is on how you can both meet the criteria and cater for mixed abilities by incorporating a range of strategies. The generic approaches are aimed at helping to stimulate your thought processes and, as a teacher, it is up to you to find ways to adapt these to suit your subject.

> *If you are struggling to link a strategy to your subject, think more widely such as the place of employment: Who would work there? What career opportunities are there for progression? Thus, how is this linked with other areas or careers where embedding maths is easier? What situations are applicable to people in any industry?*

Recognise and describe number patterns (E3)

Construction

Your students run a construction company that has a contract to build a house. However, your client states that her planning permission has now been granted and she would like to add a further nine houses. After calculating the costs for the first house, and drawing on several of the criteria already mentioned, you need to estimate an overall cost for the ten houses. If for the first house you provided an estimate of £75,000, you may need to multiply this by 10 (although you can vary the designs to raise the complexity). Show how the multiplications of 10 are situated in a pattern – i.e. if the original amount has a zero at the end then add another zero to it: 75,000 × 10 = 750,000. It is important to note here that this lesson would build on your teaching of place value.

For context and understanding, your students will need to know that the rule is not to randomly add a zero; rather, the number moves along the scale in the place value model and thus becomes ten times bigger. Consequently, the zero is significant as a value in itself. This explanation is arguably crucial as it situates the learning within the meaningful context and encourages the students to ask questions. After all, if your stretch and challenge activities have been successful, your students will want to know where the zero comes from anyway.

If you wish to start with something more simplistic, in order to develop your learners, you could price an individual brick at £2 and show how calculating a number of bricks reveals a pattern – the original number is always doubled. For instance, 50 bricks would require 2 × 50, or 150 bricks would mean 2 × 150, and so on. In this case, the pattern is formed from the price (£2), which is constant. As with other tasks, this activity can be made far more complex by introducing discounts – reductions in percentage for so many in a purchase, or buy 50, get two free, for example. Or, by revising the style of each house so that the number of bricks per house varies.

 In practice

Think about applying Bruner's (1960) concept of a spiral curriculum. Are there aspects of previous sessions you can use to reinforce what you are saying? Examples can be found in Chapter 3.

Complete simple calculations involving money and measures (E3). Work out areas and perimeters in practical situations (L1)

Building on the previous example (and this is often a good idea to cover several lessons with one major project that is multifaceted), the area and perimeter for each room may be given (level 1 learners will be expected to calculate this) with a handout of prices for flooring. So, a room is 4m² and floor tiles are £5 per box, which covers 1m². While the area and perimeter are not calculated at entry level, introducing them as measurements will ease the transition to level 1.

Dance

Your students are choreographing a performance and you feel there are too many in the group for the size of the stage and because of the level of activity involved. You agree on a general rule of five square metres per person. What is the area of your performance space? How many people will this allow? If we introduce more people, what is the area of space that is needed? Ask your students to collate the data and to draw up a chart that you can all follow. You are now branching out and into level 1, as not only are they reading and interpreting data but they are compiling it too. For perimeter, it may be useful to remember this as putting the PERson in PERimeter. If you walked around a field, how far will you have travelled by the time you get to the spot where you started? That's perimeter! Supposing your sport science students needed to calculate the white lines outlining a football pitch, or your construction workers have laid a laminate floor and now need to add the beading round the edges. These are examples of perimeter and if you put the PER into it you should be able to distinguish it from area.

Recognise and name simple 2D and 3D shapes and their properties (E3). Construct geometric diagrams, models and shapes (L1)

Art and design

Shapes are a major part of this subject and there is a strong connection between art and maths. What techniques do you employ for drawing 3D shapes? How do 2D and 3D shapes differ? What about angles? How can these help your students to understand scale and dimension?

Construction

Using a scale drawing of a building site for several new offices, your students can calculate some of the required materials for the job, such as the number of bricks and sand and cement (ratio can be considered here too). The offices are cuboid, although there is a central meeting room that is a pentagonal prism. The bricks are sold in square metres (area, again) and windows and doors will need to be accounted for, i.e. these spaces will not include any bricks. If your students are up to it, ask them to design the offices using the shapes mentioned, along with any others you feel you should add. As with all activities, vary the level according to where your students are up to but aim to challenge them whenever possible.

 ━━ Learning exercise ━━

Note down two examples in which your students can use a real-life experience for an activity that you would normally do in a lesson. For instance, in *health and social care*, you may have explored professional environments via the internet and through discussions. Could you arrange a visit to a care home to reify the experience?

Use metric units in everyday situations (E3)

Catering

Your students are baking an apple pie but the ingredients are in imperial measurements. Show them how to convert these to metric in order to follow the guidelines.

Motor vehicle mechanics

Find an old guidebook for motor mechanics and ask your students to convert any imperial measurements to metric. Alternatively, convert metric to imperial so that they can follow the instructions. While you want your students to feel challenged, you will need to facilitate the process, and make a judgement on when they need support and when they can push themselves more. How do metric units compare to real life? Speedometers are often referred to in miles per hour – as is the road system in Britain – and many notices use feet and inches: bridge signs, for instance, may say something along the lines of 14' 6".

Extract, use and compare information from lists, tables, simple charts and simple graphs (E3). Extract and interpret information from tables, diagrams, charts and graphs (L1)

Child care

Using information from government statistics and other child-centred organisations (see useful websites at the end of the chapter), ask your students to draw up a table of reported cases of neglect and abuse over the last decade.

Sport science

You show your class that the statistics for injuries in sports have risen (or reduced) in recent years. Initially, you hold a discussion about the possible causes (drawing on the criteria for English) and decide that as a group you need to decipher these statistics to identify the implications for your profession. How do they impact on your students as sportspeople? If the statistics are relevant, the students may be more inclined to take note. Find a bar chart outlining the rise (or fall) in sports injuries. Could this information be represented another way? With more details on which particular sports and types of injuries, could your students design a pie chart for each sport for the three most recent years? Or, pick two particularly significant years and compare. Averages can also be considered here too. For example, what is the average number of injuries for contact sports?

Understand and use whole numbers and understand negative numbers in practical contexts (L1/L2). Solve problems requiring calculation with common measures, including money, time, length, weight, capacity and temperature (L1). Collect and record discrete data and organise and represent information in different ways using ICT (L1/L2). Use data to assess the likelihood of an outcome (L1)

Geology

Your students are going to explore geologic temperature in an attempt to predict the next ice age. You will either present them with data from previous years or ask them to research this, depending on their level and ability. Higher-level students can work with those less capable but you will still need to be on hand to facilitate the process as the more-knowledgeable other (Vygotsky 1978). When presenting data to your students, try to find ways in which they do not appear too complex, otherwise your students may switch off. Although there is an element of data in your subject, it is likely your students will not appreciate an overload.

A temperature line is a useful way of presenting information consisting of negative and positive numbers and this can be used in various subject areas that involve temperature – cookery, physics, biology, environmental sciences. Furthermore, this strategy can be used as a timeline: history (obviously), drama (from its five theorised origins), film studies (tracing the roots of cinema – first moving image, silent era, talkies, colour and so on). Also, it can be used as gauge for height, where minus numbers may represent underground or below sea level.

The data illustrating temperatures over the years can be interpreted in many ways. Can your students draw an average for each year or century? Can they make predictions from the patterns in the data? Perhaps they can use a pie chart to represent the temperatures this century and compare this with the last two or three. You may find that temperatures before 1850 are difficult to ascertain. How does this affect your data? This can generate a discussion, particularly where there is evidence of severely low temperatures and ice ages prior to this point. For the criteria above, calculations involving money have been covered elsewhere. However, you may wish to explore the financial implications of global temperature change.

> *When we do maths, it's always related to the topic so it's enjoyable. I wasn't that good at maths at school but if they'd made it more interesting I might have been into it.*
>
> (Becca, hair and beauty student)

Raising the complexity

This section revisits some of the earlier criteria of level 1 to explore the transition to level 2. As such, it provides further examples for raising the complexity of an activity.

Find area, perimeter and volume of common shapes (L2)

Sport science

The earlier example of calculating the surface area of a swimming pool can be developed to look at volume. Who fills the pool? Is there a formula for the rate at which it is filled? How long will it take? This will impact on staffing and opening times, unless you can fill the pool in more unsociable hours. Will this require you as the manager to pay somebody overtime, however? How often does this need doing? What budgetary implications are there?

Is there a set 'safe space' for your customers to swim in? This means that the capacity of the pool will have a limitation on how many people may be using it, as well as the number of lifeguards needed. Think of ratio: one per ten persons (1:10). This activity, then, has the potential to be much larger than at first seems. As seen earlier, this is an activity you can extend over a number of weeks.

 Learning exercise

Look at the maths criteria that you are expected to deliver and draw links between several aspects of it. For instance, while you identify 3D objects, could you also incorporate volume?

Collect and represent discrete and continuous data, using ICT where appropriate; Use and interpret statistical measures, tables and diagrams, for discrete and continuous data, using ICT where appropriate; Use statistical methods to investigate situations (L2)

The most notable difference between the first criterion and that of its level 1 counterpart is the use of ICT. So, rather than duplicate the point it is sufficient to say that the representation of data in graphs can be done with a computer program. Smartdraw (see useful websites) offers free downloads (at least it did at the time of writing) but for those of you who are more proficient you could try more advanced packages to include statistics, such as SPSS or R. Here is where you can really build on your professional relationships. Consult your college's ICT person who should be able to help with free software or programs that your institution subscribes to. Developing technology-enhanced learning (TEL) is discussed further in Chapter 6.

Use probability to assess the likelihood of an outcome (L2)

Plumbing

Your students work for a large firm which has recently secured a contract for work on 22 building sites. Frank, the boss, has divided them up into four areas, one for each plumber. However, this is causing friction in the workplace as some areas will require more days and as the plumbers are self-employed the payment will therefore vary for each job. Frank decides to settle this using probability and his handy bag of sweets (that he normally has as a treat after lunch). He uses a separate coloured sweet for each area and places one sweet of that colour per job into a glass jar. There are 44 jobs in total. The breakdown is as follows:

6 yellow (Area 1), 16 blue (Area 2), 12 red (Area 3), 10 green (Area 4)

Ayesha selects first. What is the probability that she will select a job from Area 3?

The answer is $\frac{12}{44}$ which simplifies to $\frac{3}{11}$

Ayesha has a three in eleven chance of choosing a job from Area 3.

This exercise seems straightforward but, again, you can really increase the complexity. For instance, the probability changes once Ayesha has chosen as the overall number has now been reduced, albeit by only one, along with the red category (Area 3). The probability for picking another red is now 11 in 43, which means that as this reduces the probability for picking other colours rises. How many greens will have already been selected if the probability for this colour is now 5 in 19? Staying with this stage, if all the reds are gone too and the number of yellows and blues is equal, how many yellows are there? And what is the probability of picking one? It is probably not good to give you all the answers so you can ponder these questions in your own time (remember, in order to learn effectively you have to challenge yourself).

You will notice from these examples that some include figures (19) whilst others are written out (nineteen). This is not sloppiness; rather, it is a deliberate move to incorporate literacy and is a strategy that you can also employ.

Maths, then, is a significantly large and important part of our lives (indeed, it shapes our knowledge of the universe) and we ALL need it.

I have hopefully dispelled some myths throughout this book; in particular, the thinking that only certain individuals are good at maths and we are either English- or maths-capable, but not both. Not true! You **can** do maths and I hope that you now agree with me that learning it is not as difficult as first appears. Also, think of how much you already **do** know, which I have attempted to highlight in this book as well. If you are with your friends and you are going for a meal, do you have trouble splitting the bill? While there may be times where it is more complex, I would argue that this is likely to be less of a barrier than sitting in a maths class and working through division. Why? It is real life and we can relate to it. It's related to our survival because it is part of what we do so we take note, we learn quickly. If this is you, you're not alone. You are also very capable in ways that you are perhaps not recognising. Maths and English overlap in lots of ways and the next chapter will attempt to unpick the aspects of English that you can draw on in your teaching.

 # Chapter summary

There are many opportunities to embed maths within a wide variety of teaching areas and it is up to you as a teacher to draw on your creativity to find these. The examples above will hopefully stimulate this process.

This chapter has covered:

- Embedding naturally.
- Mixed abilities.
- Maths in practice.
- Raising the complexity.

References

Ausubel, DP (1968) *Educational Psychology: A Cognitive View*. New York: Holt, Rinehart and Winston Inc.

Bruner, J (1960) *The Process of Education*. Cambridge, Massachusetts: Harvard University Press.

Rose, S (1995) *Classic Film Guide*. London: Collins.

Vygotsky, L (1978) *Mind in Society*. Cambridge, Massachusetts: Harvard University Press.

Useful websites

BBC Bitesize – **www.bbc.co.uk/education/**

BBC Skillswise – **www.bbc.co.uk/skillswise/0/**

BKSB – **www.bksb.co.uk/**

Children's Society – **www.childrenssociety.org.uk/**

Free functional skills and skills for life resources – **www.skillsworkshop.org/**

Functional skills – **www.forskills.co.uk/what-are-functional-skills/**

Maths and English support – **www.maths-english.com/**

NSPCC – **www.nspcc.org.uk/**

R – **www.r-project.org/**

Resources – **www.mathsisfun.com/**

Skills for Life Network – **www.skillsforlifenetwork.com/**

Smartdraw – **www.smartdraw.com/**

SPSS – **www.ibm.com/**

5
Strategies for embedding English

This chapter

This chapter explores strategies for embedding English within a variety of subject areas. As with the chapter on embedding maths, the focus is on the *functional* aspects of English. Thus, the areas and levels looked at mirror the current functional skills criteria.

This chapter will cover:

- Level 1. Speaking, listening and communication.
- Level 1. Reading.
- Level 1. Writing.
- Level 2. Speaking, listening and communication.
- Storytelling.
- Level 2. Reading.
- Level 2. Writing.
- Justifying your embedding.
- Professionalism.
- Interdisciplinary working.

Level 1. Speaking, listening and communication

Take full part in formal and informal discussions and exchanges that include unfamiliar subjects

a) *Make relevant and extended contributions to discussions, allowing for and responding to others' input.*

b) *Prepare for and contribute to the formal discussion of ideas and opinions.*

c) *Make different kinds of contributions to discussions.*

d) *Present information/points of view clearly and in appropriate language.*

In these criteria, we can clump together the various sections as they form an overall focus. This helps considerably as it means that you can generate a project for your students that will run over a number of weeks. Within your teaching, if you have scope to initiate a debate – and all good education programmes would facilitate this opportunity, given the value we should arguably place on cognition, reflection and metacognition – then this can stimulate interest in a variety of ways. The significance of debates is that when they work, they 'really' work. Personalities may emerge in ways that you possibly couldn't imagine, and to see this fiery passion in action is both exciting and rewarding. This is perhaps the stage you wish for in your teaching: the students' full-on engagement with *your* planned lesson.

Learning exercise

Identify five instances in the English specification that resonate with your subject area.

First, what is current in your area? Are there any naturally occurring concerns that arise? For instance, you may teach an industrial-related subject and can foresee significant changes in the coming years as the implications of Brexit become apparent. Do your learners understand possible consequences? Consider these implications for your debate and decide upon a topic. Is the class split on your topic? If so, you can glean individual points of view. If you find that they are mostly on one side, ask them to assume a counter argument for the debate, even if it goes against what they feel. Attempting to defend something you do not believe in is difficult so you may need to help them. However, point out that it is only role playing and that it can develop a deeper understanding of the opposing view, which is often a key factor in strengthening your own argument. In this way, you can assess your students on their ability to 'respond appropriately to others' point of view' and to 'follow the main points of discussions'.

Moreover, this can lead to opportunities to probe your students further to really stretch and challenge them. Why do they have this viewpoint? What evidence is it based on? Is this thinking influenced by culture? What other factors could you bring in? For instance, relate it to equality and diversity as you explore varying cultural contexts and perceptions. Who, or what, are the influences on their beliefs and decisions? You may need to provide some contextual information so that your students can make an informed choice.

In practice

Engineering

Half of your group run a large engineering organisation that builds, and services, military aeroplanes. The company used to draw heavily on European trade but now relations are strained. The other half run a small family business providing engineering parts to customers across the UK. They are beginning to develop their clientele base as Brexit negotiations are implemented and claim that they have suffered from heavy taxation through membership of the EU. This is merely a starting point and you can provide further details as you build the complexity of the debate to suit your students' abilities.

Your role in the debate may be facilitator, or you may feel that a mediator is required. As the debate grows, however, you will need to sustain control of the group and guide them on an appropriate course. What strategies will you draw on to 'clarify and confirm understanding?' Could you ask (or allocate) each person to take a specific argument and to present this to the opposition for around one minute? Can they identify three aspects of why they feel their argument is right? In assessing for 'appropriate language' use, what do you deem to be appropriate, and why? Do your students understand this? Is there a gulf between your perception and that of others?

Working with language in this way can develop your teaching in other ways. You may become more aware of terminology and conceptualisations used and this will help to improve your gauge of whether your students have understood what is required of them. While you cannot measure understanding per se, you can make a subjective assessment of it through performance, i.e. your students' ability to demonstrate the objectives of the debate (or other activity). *For relevant contributions,* again, you need to make a judgement call on what you feel is 'relevant' but you can steer the debate by posing direct questions so that specific responses are called for.

Whilst this is mostly self-explanatory – find a topic and debate it – you may wish to think further afield than your subject, particularly in relation to what is known as enhancement opportunities, or 'extra-curricular' teaching. Do you run sessions on 'academic writing' or 'managing your time?' Can these feed into a debate once the content is covered? Furthermore, a debate will also enable you to incorporate other policy focuses that are currently relevant. For instance, you could initiate a discussion around FBV (fundamental British values). What is it? Why is it important? What is Britishness? Is there a consensus in the group or disharmony? How can you utilise this disharmony (being mindful of extreme views, of course) to its full effect?

Learning exercise

Drama

In groups of three, you tell your students, *you are going to get up and conduct an improvisation in a Brechtian manner to illustrate Epic theatre. I will give you instructions and you will respond, and act, according to what I say. However, you cannot present it naturalistically.* This can be done for most subjects with the medium of drama merely fuelling the activity. For instance, you could ask them to act out a customer–client scenario in a Brechtian style where they 'break the fourth wall' and address the audience (or camera).

Regardless of your subject, you can easily fulfil the listening aspect of this section through giving instructions. Ask your class to listen carefully while you work your way through a guided, and sequential, process of instructions relating to a specific activity within your area. For instance, you might try a drama activity (see example boxes) for your performers. Working in groups is usually good to avoid putting a student on the spot, but it also allows you to pinpoint individuals if you need to.

Learning exercise

Business studies

Your students have initiated a range of business ideas and now need to look into setting these up. You can list the process that they need to record but for greater effect you will want to discuss the implications of each stage and ask for ideas on how to deal with each one. This can draw on a questioning process, such as the *Pose, Pause, Pounce, Bounce* (PPPB).

There are many strategies for posing questions to your students but from experience PPPB is an effective tool for promoting assessment for learning. PPPB has been popularised by Dylan Wiliam and is said to be originally attributed to a teacher called Mrs Pam Fearnley (McGill, 2011).

In this activity, you *pose* a question, *pause* to allow your students to process it, *pounce* (not literally) on your chosen student, and then *bounce* that response across the class, i.e. choose another person to respond. This is a great technique for initiating discussions and for eliciting views, but it also enables you to target specific students with appropriate questions, while ensuring that everyone in the class feels included. Furthermore, the students are encouraged to listen, as they do not know who the 'bounce' will fall on next.

You can also move the questioning on to allow for differentiation. For instance, you begin with a straightforward question, one that is within the ability level of a particular student but will require them to ponder it (or perhaps you know that this student needs to develop their confidence and self-esteem and will answer it easily) and then you raise the level of complexity of the question for another student.

In practice

Example of PPPB

Film studies

Teacher: Johnny, what was the highest grossing film of last year?

Johnny: [names film]

Teacher: Yes, good. Ranji, what percentage of its profit was from merchandise? (embedding maths!)

Ranji: [gives answer]

Teacher: Excellent. Elizabeth, give me two typical elements of mise en scène for this film.

This is a seemingly natural progression and looks like you are merely exploring the film (which, of course, you are); however, the questioning level is layered.

Level 1. Reading

Read and understand a range of straightforward texts.

a) *Identify the main points and ideas and how they are presented in a variety of texts.*

b) *Read and understand texts in detail.*

c) *Utilise information contained in texts.*

d) *Identify suitable responses to texts.*

e) *In more than one type of text.*

Archaeology

You have a series of texts from academic journals, newspaper articles, reputable websites, professional forums and blogs that cover several key discoveries in the field of archaeology. There are a variety of viewpoints in the texts as well as factual information and the spread of information you present to your class is diverse. Split the class into several groups of three and ask them to choose a text. They will be required to generate meaning from the texts and then to deliver this back to the whole class. Ask them to present their ideas in a variety of ways – this could be in the form of a mind map or something more simplistic such as bullet points. The main aspect, however, is that they are drawing out the relevant information.

For the sources, the content will vary and you can use this for differentiation – perhaps giving more complex texts to those working at a higher level. The next step from each subgroup is to ask them to discuss the implications of the text for archaeology. For example, you may have an article on the recent (2012) archaeological find of the skeleton of King Richard III. Your students will piece together the information and elicit what they believe the text is saying. Consequently, they should be in a position to consider the implications this will have for the field as a whole. How do your students feel it will impact on them as future archaeologists? Does such a find generate greater funding? Does it expand the potential for more finds? What are the implications for the University of Leicester, for the key academics involved and for the city of Leicester?

 In practice

Thinking about Lave and Wenger's (2009) concept of legitimate peripheral participation, can you identify those students in the debate who are perhaps on the periphery? What strategies can you identify that make them more heavily included? Although this is a snapshot of a more complex concept, you may be able to observe one or two of your students engaging with the community of practice on a superficial level. This should help you to think about how you can facilitate the process where your students move into the community of practice of their future profession.

As you can see, this can lead you into several aspects of the speaking and listening criteria and there is no reason why you cannot combine the two over a number of sessions, perhaps extending the project to accommodate this. Furthermore, depending on the content and your particular focus within your teaching, you may want to extend this again with a writing exercise. Writing is a way of consolidating learning and we shall look at the criteria for this next.

Level 1. Writing

Write a range of texts to communicate information, ideas and opinions, using formats and styles suitable for their purpose and audience.

a) Write clearly and coherently, including an appropriate level of detail.

b) Present information in a logical sequence.

c) Use language, format and structure suitable for purpose and audience.

d) Use correct grammar, including correct and consistent use of tense.

e) Ensure written work includes generally accurate punctuation and spelling and that meaning is clear.

f) In more than one type of text.

Most of us will be familiar with essays and written assignments – usually conceptualised as the 'academic stuff'. However, this can be misleading in that it may degrade, or miscategorise, other forms of learning. For instance, reflective accounts are often useful in that students can draw out personal information, and this can generate writing that is of a more free-flowing style, rather than a mechanistic way of regurgitating and reformatting existing information. Reflective writing can be formalised, too, including grammatically sound sentences and academic references; it does not need to include slang or other unusual phraseology merely because that is how we may think or speak.

There are many styles of writing and this opens up possibilities for teaching. For example, your students could engage in a blog debate, where posts are dialogic. That is, they consist of multiple sources of information in a process of exchange as a concern or idea is explored. Although this is a form of writing in itself, you may decide you don't want to end it there and the blog could act as leverage for other writing. For instance, the information could be used as a foundation for an essay or a report.

 In practice

Religious studies

What religious stories can you think of? The Plagues of Egypt? Could you go back in time and record the events in your diary as you bear witness to them? Perhaps you could assume some leading figure of the period instead and write from their perspective? Or, you are a Muslim about to embark on the hajj, a pilgrimage that will take you to Mecca. What have you had to do to ensure that this journey was possible? How will it affect your life afterwards? What do your friends feel about you undertaking the hajj?

You may feel that most creative activities in writing seem more appealing to primary school children; if so, you should rethink this. Most of us love a bit of an adventure, and the opportunity to indulge in some creativity. Perhaps your students are historical detectives, piecing together the bits of information to generate a twenty-first-century interpretation on the events? The creativity is up to you but it is important to see that the criteria for English can fit in almost any subject's syllabus. What is required is your creative ability to make the connection. Much of religious teaching, for instance, is based on scripts and requires analysis, evaluation and interpretation. These scripts are forms of literature and can be subjected to many of the textual analyses that you would apply to other key texts as you explore interpretation.

 In practice

Tell your students that they are journalists writing about their recent visit to the Western (Wailing) Wall. They will need to incorporate the diversity of views associated with the wall and the various claims that have been made, including historical evidence from the key religious perspectives. Some research will most likely be involved, although this lesson would be most beneficial once you have covered this topic in the syllabus.

Level 2. Speaking, listening and communication

Make a range of contributions to discussions in a range of contexts, including those that are unfamiliar, and make effective presentations.

a) *Consider complex information and give a relevant, cogent response in appropriate language.*

b) *Present information and ideas clearly and persuasively to others.*

c) *Adapt contributions to suit audience, purpose and situation.*

d) *Make significant contributions to discussions, taking a range of roles and helping to move discussion forward.*

Hot-seating is an enjoyable and rewarding activity that you can do with your students. They will need to choose, and assume the guise of, a character – perhaps you are studying history and there are several characters of interest – for role playing. In the hot seat, the character tells us about themselves in one minute and then responds to questions. The questions may vary and be seemingly random as the aim is to stimulate deeper thinking. For instance, you are an apothecary caring for the sick in medieval Britain. You treated a man yesterday evening and his health unfortunately deteriorated. *What factors do you believe caused this? What is your opinion on the medicines used?* From this conversation, you may be able to elicit some of the cultural influences and supernatural beliefs that would have impacted on treatment.

In practice

Room 101, now seen on TV with Frank Skinner. Your student has three items to select that they would like to see put in Room 101. (For those interested, the concept originates from George Orwell's novel, *1984*. Room 101 was an unspoken place of horror, a room you would end up in if the authority wanted to dispose of you.) They then argue their case and as tutor, you will have the overall decision of whether that item goes in there. It is a very effective activity – particularly now that Frank Skinner is popularising it on the BBC – and you can incorporate it in most lessons. For instance, what three features of being a professional plumber would you like to dispose of?

Often, the biggest challenge is restricting the list to three items but you may need to help your students, such as by initiating a discussion about professionalism to stimulate thinking. For feedback, ask your students to pick three aspects of the course that niggle them.

Storytelling

Storytelling is also often an effective way of meeting the criteria for speaking and although this may look difficult to incorporate at first, particularly if you teach something like electrical installation, it is more straightforward than it seems. Without wishing to stereotype, what tradesperson doesn't have a good story? Most of us engage in storytelling in lots of ways and we love to relate events in the form of a story. Listen to your friends informing you of the latest incident in their lives or their recent mishaps. Do they merely say, 'I' scratched the bumper of my car this morning'? In many situations, your friend will recount the event in the form of a narrative; perhaps not directly after the event, but after some time has passed, this incident usually becomes a story.

Your friend may begin by telling you how the day was a typical one and they had left the house as usual; maybe there were some thoughts at the forefront of their mind that dominate the story. Whatever the events, look for the narrative. We are natural storytellers and it is something that we do well. Therefore, you can utilise this in your teaching. Give your students a scenario, preferably a real-life one for context and to generate greater empathy between them and the people involved in the situation.

Geography

In early September 2016, an earthquake hit the north island of New Zealand, with a rippling 7.1 magnitude. The country is said to be home to thousands of earthquakes per year, albeit only a comparatively small number will be felt by the general public. However, this does mean that it is a potential talking point for your class and one that can be used for generating a case study. Within your subject you will explore the reasons for earthquakes and the consequences – tsunamis, lost homes, urban destruction, and even death – and real-life cases are always meaningful and thus useful to examine (although you will need to know your class well and to consider how such a sensitive issue may evoke unwanted emotions for those of your students who feel a connection to the area – again, this is a judgement call).

Generally, your students will like the idea that they are in touch with real-life events and that they are learning about how their subject area interacts with the world around them. In this way, the criteria for English is deeply embedded and the focus appears to be on the geographical elements, such as gaining an understanding of earthquakes and tsunamis (and of course whatever else this scenario impacts on within the remit of the geography syllabus). Information can be given to your students in a variety of ways. You may use the interactive whiteboard, Prezi or something more sophisticated that will engage your learners (see Chapter 6) or even good old-fashioned handouts (they haven't died yet) and these can include numbers, such as statistics, which means you can also bring in maths – calculating the mean and mode for the magnitudes, for example, or drawing a graph to represent them.

The students' task is to reformat the layout of the information into a narrative. The information may have extracts of voices or a mixture of several sources and these should include features of writing that you can introduce to your students and ask them to discuss, such as bullet points, structured paragraphs, facts and opinions, direct quotes and so on. You can also incorporate a range of stylistic elements of writing, such as argument, persuasion and advice. Your students will need to consider how they interpret the text(s) and then how they will re-present the information to their peers. As you are looking for them to generate a story from the material, you will need to vary the sources to generate a variety of viewpoints.

Finally, the groups will need to consider a way forward for the situation. What happens next? What support needs can be identified? How will this be facilitated and who will be involved? Allocate a role for each member in the group so that you can gauge their input. At the end of the activity, ask each group to present what they have found to the class. In this way, you can assess them against the criteria. Have they taken the 'complex information' and provided 'a relevant, cogent response in appropriate language?' Is the information presented 'clearly and persuasively to others?' In what way have they adapted the information 'to suit audience, purpose and situation?' Do they identify key strategies for resolution? How significant is their overall contribution? Does it move the argument on or arrive at a plausible conclusion?

A useful resource

As a teacher, anecdotal accounts are not something that you would present as evidence but students usually respond positively to them. They illustrate that you have a life outside teaching, but that you also have lots of knowledge of the field, and that they (your students) can learn from your professional experience. Draw on your own professional anecdotes as exemplary material for what your students can do with information. These will likely be more interesting than generic ones and your students will usually embrace them as they want to gain a realistic insight into the industry. Present them as stories and incorporate strategies for persuasion.

Level 2. Reading

Select, read, understand and compare texts and use them to gather information, ideas, arguments and opinions.

a) Select and use different types of texts to obtain and utilise relevant information.

b) Read and summarise, succinctly, information/ideas from different sources.

c) Identify the purposes of texts and comment on how meaning is conveyed.

d) Detect point of view, implicit meaning and/or bias.

e) Analyse texts in relation to audience needs and consider suitable responses.

f) In three or more texts.

Level 2 focuses more on 'implicit meaning' and analysis and thus requires the students to demonstrate deeper knowledge and understanding than level 1. It builds on the skills acquired in the previous level but then adds a dimension of criticality. This will be more in line with your course if you are teaching at level 2 and above. As such, you may be able to cross-reference the criteria to match the learning outcomes. Thus, it is likely that you will have a clearer idea of the expectations at level 2. Perhaps most importantly, how do your students' views differ and what conclusions do they reach?

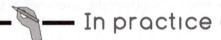 In practice

Psychology

Select two studies that you can compare. Perhaps one states that children learn more effectively through individual exploration, while another promotes social learning and a purely collaborative approach. Ask your students to identify the strengths and weaknesses and to reach a conclusion. How much of the texts can they illustrate as 'point of view' or 'implicit meaning?' What is the purpose of each? How do the authors argue their point? What strategies do they use? Is one text more persuasive because it is supported by stronger, more robust, data? Is the author voice clear?

Almost any theory is good in that it is yet to be (dis)proved. You could even take something as contentious as learning styles (but perhaps not brain gym). Have a look at Frank Coffield *et al*.'s (2004) marvellous 'chainsaw' critique. Is that clean-cut enough? What do your students think? At this level, ensure that the reading materials either you provide or the students find are sufficiently critical enough to generate deep responses. You will need to evidence how you believe they have demonstrated knowledge and understanding at the appropriate level. Think carefully about your assessment and if in doubt draw on any of the strategies outlined in this book.

Level 2. Writing

Write a range of texts, including extended written documents, communicating information, ideas and opinions effectively and persuasively.

a) Present information/ideas concisely, logically and persuasively.

b) Present information on complex subjects clearly and concisely.

c) Use a range of writing styles for different purposes.

d) *Use a range of sentence structures, including complex sentences, and paragraphs to organise written communication effectively.*

e) *Punctuate written text using commas, apostrophes and inverted commas accurately.*

f) *Ensure written work is fit for purpose and audience, with accurate spelling and grammar that support clear meaning in a range of text types.*

The specification for writing at level 2 is quite similar to level 1, albeit there is an expectation for evidence of more complexity. For instance, apostrophes, commas and complex sentences are now mentioned, and spelling is required to be 'accurate' rather than 'generally accurate'. The scenarios described earlier, then, are highly relevant, although the content and assessment would need to reflect the level 2 criteria. With a bit of tweaking, and higher expectations, this is easily achievable. However, just to be clear, there is another example in the box below.

 ── In practice ──────

Health and social care

Your students are going to write about mental health and developing from level 1 means they are required to research it. Research - referring here to 'background reading' rather than an actual research project - moves the work up a level because it helps to situate it within the field in a more academic manner. This reading will help your students to write in a 'range of text types'.

Introduce your students to a variety of sources and discuss the merits of each before asking them to use some of these resources for their argument. You might decide on an argument beforehand and then encourage the students to take up a viewpoint, having read the resources. Or, if you feel that your students can handle the challenge, ask them to explore the resources and then to summarise them, before eventually generating an argument from what they have read.

Justifying your embedding

Strange as it may seem, reading is an integral part of writing. All good writers are keen readers; this is not a natural ability, evident at birth. Writing – like learning – is about exposure, or what is more usually termed experience. The more we engage with written materials the more we will assimilate, which will thus inform our writing. Your students, then, will need to adopt these practices. This may appear obvious but often the connection is not made by students. They do know, however, that they would not be expected to write an essay for your subject if they had not studied it. The same applies for personal experiences. How much have they had? Do they mostly rely on rumours or verbal accounts of the world? Can you help them to think critically? If you are teaching English literature, this is part and parcel of what you do. If you teach plastering, this may not be so explicit. It is just as relevant, however, and it is up to you to help your students to understand its importance.

> *'Why do we need to write about plastering? That won't make the wall look any better?'*

Professionalism

Aside from an exercise in employability, your students will need to market themselves as assets in a competitive world. Do they have a CV? Is it littered with misspellings and grammatical infelicities? What image does this give off? Perceptions of professionalism will undoubtedly affect their future. Is shoddy paperwork a sign of shoddy workmanship? Perhaps! It will certainly be seen that way by many people. If you are training to be a teacher (or have already trained), you will know about the importance of professionalism. Your lecturers were not espousing, and consistently reaffirming, all those messages for nothing, as I'm sure you have come to realise. It is now *your* turn, *your* job to pass the message on to *your* students. English and maths *are* important. And don't let them forget it.

Interdisciplinary working

While English and maths have been discussed as separate chapters, they are very much interrelated and there will be many opportunities to embed both, often in the same activity. For instance, as mentioned earlier the use of a debate for thrashing out concerns in your chosen area (also good for developing employability and professional knowledge) and for incorporating, and raising awareness of, the wider remit of the sector (think of Prevent, safeguarding, FBV and so on) can be a starting point for further activities, such as presenting the argument in a report and drawing on statistics to support it. Alternatively, the debate itself may have emanated from an analysis of data. As a teacher embedding these areas, then, you should think about ways you can draw on maths and English together. And, most importantly, how they can complement, and are arguably essential in, your subject area.

 Chapter summary

English, particularly in the form of literacy, can be embedded in most subjects as it mostly draws on what we do daily. A large majority of us use language to communicate through reading and writing and we rely on English skills to achieve this effectively. Therefore, embedding requires an element of creativity to incorporate what we are generally cognisant of, and to develop this to meet the requirements of our subject.

This chapter has covered:

- Level 1. Speaking, listening and communication.
- Level 1. Reading.
- Level 1. Writing.
- Level 2. Speaking, listening and communication.

- Storytelling.
- Level 2. Reading.
- Level 2. Writing.
- Justifying your embedding.
- Professionalism.
- Interdisciplinary working.

References

Coffield, F, Moseley, D, Hall, E and Ecclestone, K (2004) *Should We Be Using Learning Styles? What Research Has to Say to Practice*. London: Learning & Skills Research Centre.

Lave, J and Wenger, E (2009) *Situated Learning: Legitimate Peripheral Participation*. Cambridge: Cambridge University Press.

McGill, RM (2011) How to move your lessons from good to outstanding. *The Guardian Online*. Available at: **www.theguardian.com/teacher-network/2011/nov/17/lessons-good-to-outstanding-afl-questioning**

Useful websites

BBC Bitesize – **www.bbc.co.uk/education/**

BBC Skillswise – **www.bbc.co.uk/skillswise/0/**

BKSB – **www.bksb.co.uk/**

Free functional skills and skills for life resources – **www.skillsworkshop.org/**

Functional skills – **www.forskills.co.uk/what-are-functional-skills/**

Functional skills resources – **http://shop.niace.org.uk/catalogsearch/advanced/result/?name=functional+skills&author=&subject=&type=&year=&search.x=27&search.y=4&search=Search**

Maths and English support – **www.maths-english.com/**

Skills for Life Network – **www.skillsforlifenetwork.com/**

6

Technology-enhanced learning

 ——— This chapter ———

This chapter explores the use of information and communication technology (ICT) to improve the learning experience and to enhance opportunities for incorporating English and maths through technology-enhanced learning (TEL). It also draws on the role of social media as a strategy for developing English and maths skills and for relating to the modern learner. Technology-enhanced learning is a powerful tool within your teaching arsenal, as it is relevant and topical. Furthermore, TEL plays a major role in many people's lives, and it is not merely a gimmick or teaching fad; it can be used to stimulate your students in ways that are relevant to them and can thus increase engagement in learning. If used appropriately, TEL can contribute to enhanced learning and can encourage deeper thinking and metacognition.

This chapter will cover:

- Digital learners.
- Technology to support employability.
- Technology and fun: whenever the twain meet, the power of teaching is at your feet.
- Tools for learning.
- Virtual learning environments (VLEs).
- Flipped classroom.
- Safeguarding and e-safety.

Digital learners

According to Marc Prensky, we are moving (or have moved) into a nation of digital learners. Prensky (2001, p2) uses the term 'digital native' to describe those individuals who are born into this life – the young people who do not remember the first time they searched the internet, often because it was there before they were born. For many adults, however, technology has grown throughout their lives and they have had to adapt to this, making them 'digital immigrants' (Prensky, 2001, p2). Since Prensky, other writers have attempted to draw on similar labels for young people who are in touch with technology, such as 'Generation Y' (Weiler, 2005) and the 'i-Generation' (Rosen, 2010) but the argument for being aware of technology and using it in your teaching remains.

Prensky (2001) radically claimed (although he later toned down this claim) that brains were changing in response to the vast exposure to technology such as the internet, mobile phones (now smartphones) and video games. However, such change is dramatic and rather anti-evolutionary. Young people are arguably no more genetically akin to technology than older generations. For a more objective perspective, however, we have to accept that for now there is no robust evidence that the brains of young people are in any way developing differently to those of older generations (Helsper and Eynon, 2010). We all have a similar capacity to learn and to evolve (and I'm not convinced evolution works that quickly), but there is much truth to the claim that young people will often have far more technological exposure and, as such, will seemingly adopt it much faster. Twenty-first-century teaching, then, arguably needs to acknowledge and complement such exposure and technological familiarity to meet varied interests.

 ## Learning exercise

Conduct a short survey with your class to see how many hours of an evening are spent on their phones/laptops/iPads/tablets and so on. Put the information into a table in Word. Can you use this to inform your teaching? What motivates your students?

Furthermore, the economic implications of using TEL are broad and its deeper embedment becomes necessary if young people are to move smoothly into the twenty-first-century workplace. Technology can boost teaching methods as it provides an important link with social media, particularly as it is often perceived as a form of entertainment, rather than linked to teaching. You can therefore use technology as a hook for engagement – drawing on it in innovative ways that can stimulate interest and enthusiasm. Moreover, it is becoming more and more common for young people to read off a screen, rather than from a paper-based resource, so it is likely that non-use of technology is in many ways alien to majority practice.

For many years following Prensky's paper, a discourse that permeated many schools was that education could no longer equip young people for the world ahead, mostly because it was unknown territory. Technology was believed to be moving so fast that the skills students had upon leaving were almost invalid by the time they arrived in the job market. This thinking means that we cannot really teach young people in the best way because we just don't know what will happen; however, this is not necessarily so. There are many skills that a young person will be introduced to throughout their life and some of these will be advanced but that does not mean that their education has left them ill-equipped. A base of skills and knowledge in English, maths, the arts and ICT will undoubtedly stand the test of time because such skills and knowledge will develop with the person and with their experiences. In this way, the student will grow into their new role in life, adapting prior knowledge and adopting the experiences that lie ahead.

Moreover, most technological advances are built on previous technological knowledge and their operationalisation often shares a practical base with existing functionality. In addition, many companies will hold back on radical changes to software/hardware to sell more products and to allow for a natural progression, and hunger, in the market. Changes, then, are small in comparison to what they could be and it is arguable that young people with the skills and experiences they already have – providing some form of TEL has been used in their learning – will be able to move with these changes. Technology is particularly important for education as it can provide that base for development. It is also arguably essential in that it may be the only area where some young people can access it. Students of low socio-economic status, for instance, may not be able to surf the internet of an evening or engage with the latest smartphones/iPads/tablets and this can be a serious disadvantage.

Technology to support employability

Clark and Formby (2013: 3) claim that *employers want young people who are literate, numerate, communicate well and possess the right attitude or work ethic*. As an FE teacher, it is likely that you are in the business of preparing young people for employment of some sort (even if this is via higher education). Whilst you may be doing a fantastic job in your vocational area, the wider remit of skills young people need to become more employable is essential in today's competitive job market. Education is not solely about moving into employment, of course, but it will certainly be high on the agenda for many young people, particularly as they transition into the adult world. Furthermore, policy pressures from government have identified these skills as essential aspects of teaching and learning in FE.

 Learning exercise

Incorporate CV writing in one of your sessions and try to address the following:

- Spelling.
- Grammar and syntax.
- Vocabulary.
- Apostrophe use.

In 2013, a survey by the Prince's Trust (2013, p2) found that one in ten young people *claim their computer skills have let them down more than their maths or English when applying for jobs*. Furthermore, Clark and Formby (2013, p3) found that young people, *feel that they are being held back in finding employment because of a lack of digital literacy.* The world of FE prepares many young people for employment, particularly where a vocational area is undertaken, and employability is a major concern for most institutions. Indeed, it is perhaps only fair that you empower your students by equipping them with the skills to compete in the job market and society in general. As said earlier, education's remit is arguably wider than the mere move into employment, but education for education's sake is unfortunately a luxury in England today as fees are currently at the feet of the individual contributor. Therefore, empowerment becomes more about choice and facilitating skills in maths and English, and other employable aspects in your students, can enable this choice.

Clark and Formby (2013, p7) claim that *young people are also now joining the workforce with technological knowledge that is often far beyond that of the generation before them at a time when the workplace itself is becoming increasingly technology-driven.* Technology, then, is very much a driving force of various forms of employment and whether you perceive your students to be digital 'natives' or 'immigrants', this will undoubtedly impact on your teaching.

 Learning exercise

List your top three strengths and three areas for development that you have in relation to technology. How would you rate yourself on a scale of 1-10?

Technology and fun: whenever the twain meet, the power of teaching is at your feet

The purpose of incorporating TEL in your teaching is to inject a little fun in your lessons, as well as adding relevance and potentially deeper meaning for your students. Technology engrosses young people in many ways and usually for a significant part of their day. It is one of their preferred methods of engagement. If you doubt this, try delivering a boring lecture to your students and see what they do. Most young people do not suffer fools, so it will not be long before the comments start. In most instances, however, a number of them will turn to technology (mobile phone?) in order to fill the void. You will need to address this in your teaching so rather than meet it head on, why not embrace it? If your students cannot go an hour without their electronic fix then you can use this to your advantage. You know that they really concentrate when they are on WhatsApp or Snapchat (or whatever is appropriate for your time of reading) and you would love to have even 50 per cent of that focus. So don't push it away. And if you want to look particularly cool (or is it 'sick'?), try to find an app that your students are not aware of.

Incorporating technology and social media apps can add an extra dimension to your teaching. It can generate greater student interactivity and can open up opportunities for you to facilitate learning. Discovery learning, for instance, can provide a base for your students to engage in an activity; however, for greatest effect, you need to be involved and facilitate the process, rather than relying on their mere exploration (although this depends on the nature of your students). The main message that should come from this chapter is that you need to do a recent search and see what technology is available and how it can be used. For now, let's have a look at how TEL can work in practice.

You are teaching fashion and retail and have decided to embed maths to help your students understand and interpret data. You present the class with a problem-based question to initiate the discovery learning process and then divide them into groups.

You are the manager of a store in a local retail park and need to evaluate your store's performance through its profit and loss accounts and wage expenditure.

Depending on the level, you can give your students all the figures and ask them to produce an appropriate graph or chart to represent the incomings and outgoings and then to conduct an analysis to see where expenditure can be reduced. Alternatively, you can ask them to Google average wages or look at existing companies where information is freely available. If each group presents what they have found, you will also be drawing on speaking and listening, grammar and punctuation in the way that they have laid the information out (perhaps on a Prezi or PowerPoint) and spelling for key words and so on, as well as developing their technological expertise.

 Learning exercise

Using the data collected from your survey, find a video on YouTube that illustrates how to turn these into a graph using Excel. If you are unfamiliar with Excel, perhaps start with Word and see what you can do. If possible, use the data to generate an analysis. You can ask your students to convert your table into various formats to present the data in a variety of ways.

Tools for learning

Below is a small number of examples of some of the many tools that can be used to incorporate TEL and further exploration is strongly encouraged as there are many, many more available.

Vox populi

This is a great use of TEL and students usually enjoy the process of interviewing others. Moreover, creating a short video will give you something to assess in addition to observing the students undertaking the activity, and they can embed the video in a Word document or upload it to a share point. In your fashion and retail lesson, it's time to do some market research on a pair of unisex trousers that your students are looking to market. If you have access to a media department, you may be able to borrow equipment that will give this a professional look. If not, digital cameras can be just as good and what resonates with students even more is using their mobile phones.

 Learning exercise

Is your video appropriate for uploading to YouTube? If you decide to do this, make sure you have obtained all the relevant permissions from those involved.

Set up a Vox pop where they are going to conduct brief interviews with other students in the college to ascertain views and to assess the market. Tell your students that they can only ask four questions, so these will have to be decided by the whole group. After brainstorming a series of questions, divide the class into groups of two and each group will have one question that they will need to argue the validity of in a debate. What is strong about the question? How does it relate to the saleability of the product? How is it more relevant than some of the others that have been presented? This will help you to further explore the speaking and listening criteria for embedding English. Once your questions have been established, and the Vox pops have been conducted, your students can collate the information into a graph, bar chart, pie chart, or whatever seems most appropriate. You may decide to give each comment a numerical value if you are looking at significance.

You can then run some basic data analysis which could involve calculating the mean, mode and so on. More advanced analysis, such as entering the data into SPSS (Statistical Package for the Social Sciences), will allow you to stretch those students who need greater challenging. This lesson, then, will draw on a wide variety of skills as it incorporates English, maths and TEL as well as your vocational area. Furthermore, are there any skills for employability that you can identify? Hopefully, as you start to unpick the content you will see that your regular teaching sessions have so much potential for growth. If you find the content is too advanced, you can always look at more fundamental uses of TEL. Did the students take the e-mail addresses of the people they interviewed? Perhaps they could send out a thank you to each one? The level of activity, then, will vary and having your students work in groups will enable them to learn from each other and to allocate suitable roles.

WhatsApp

It is likely that you will not be introducing this application to your students; rather, you are drawing on something they will probably already be familiar with. However, you are showing that you speak their language, so to speak, and it breaks up the dynamics of the lesson by mixing the home–college balance.

Business studies

Ask your students to investigate some of the causes of small business failure in the first two years and to write the findings in the form of a short report (500 words). Split them into small groups of six members and then three subgroups (two people in each). The students can undertake different elements of the research in their groups of two but later come together as the larger group to write up the findings. They can therefore use the WhatsApp to share the findings of their research and to stay in communication as they work in their smaller groups. Throughout the process, they can upload images and raise questions for others to tackle – such as, how do these findings compare to the section of the report you are looking at? What strategies do more-successful businesses employ to stay afloat? In this way, the students communicate and collaborate throughout. For the report, they can build in reflection through their free writing and WhatsApp can be further used to provide a link to a blog or posting where the report can be accessed. Thus, this app can work well with other tools for TEL.

— Learning exercise

Introduce the following sentence from a blog post and ask your students to correct the grammatical errors:

> We went throu the activity with Edwina this morning and the hole class said that there ideas would work better if we had a student voice, Edwina agreed to, so did the panel, we decided as a class we would establish a forum for erring alot of views; Jemima said she is happy for it to be lead by her.

If you do not have a WhatsApp account that can be shared with the students, you could e-mail this to one student and ask them to WhatsApp it so that the rest of the class can access it.

Animoto and PowToon

Animoto and PowToon are great for making videos in a really short time and can incorporate many technological skills. Videos can promote ideas, beliefs, products and so on and thus interlink with other subject areas. Supposing your motor vehicle mechanic students are looking at promoting their vocational area to next year's students. They can make, and star in, a video that illustrates their work. You can also incorporate English and maths, such as devising an accompanying narrative (with terms specific to motor vehicle mechanics) and perhaps produce a graph showing where previous students have progressed to.

Twitter

Sports studies

Ask your students to set up a Twitter account to deliver sport updates for the college basketball team. There is a difficult league game coming up and the team are a player down. An appeal tweet is needed. Include a photo taken from the previous match and generate a hashtag so the followers can keep up to date with the results of future matches. Encourage postings to have varied sentence lengths and structure: simple, complex, compound. Are they grammatically correct? Have they been proofread for misspellings?

Facebook

Most colleges will have a Facebook account and students often devise their own one to represent their group. If you are a training teacher, you may have done this yourself so you will be aware of the benefits (and drawbacks). Facebook is a great way to get to your students quickly, as most will have it on their phones. Moreover, despite the classroom environment involving face-to-face communication, there is usually greater uptake of requests when this is used. It may be the fun element or the fact that they can reply while watching the TV so their lives are not disturbed too much.

Film studies

You post a clip of a controversial film on the college's Facebook wall (or group's if you are a part – more on the safety of this later) and ask for comments on mise en scène. The level of guidance you give your students will depend on how well you know them and their ability, and what you are hoping to achieve from the exercise. Your students may generate a forum for discussing the film or merely comment on other students' words. You might even decide to a do a pose, pause, pounce, bounce (see Chapter 5) style of commenting, where you add to the comments yourself and then direct the next one to a particular student.

A Facebook account is also a good way to keep your students connected socially and this can further develop relationships that have been built in the classroom. Furthermore, if there is a general query that concerns the whole group, you can either post it on Facebook or ask a student to share the information for you. A strong caveat to using Facebook and, indeed, any other form of TEL, is the monitoring of online bullying (for safeguarding) and your own involvement, which can impact on professionalism. It is advisable to avoid linking your personal account to students as this can put you in an invidious position (in all sorts of ways you may not have envisaged) and, in many instances, may be breaching your institution's policy in some way. Another down-side is that your teaching role can change dramatically, with your usual working hours being stretched considerably. While it is great to support your students beyond the institution, this can impact on your health and well-being if taken to excess; therefore, you will need to ensure that you have an effective work–life balance. This will also impact on your teaching in the classroom and you will soon be doing more damage than good, despite the fact that you are putting in far more hours.

> I couldn't get through my PGCE without the Facebook page. It's how we communicate ... it's how we draw on each other for a bit of moral support. If one of us has a problem, it gets posted on Facebook and someone usually responds. That's what we need when we're not in uni.
>
> (Karin, PGCE student)

Coggle

For those of you who like mind maps or just generally prefer to see a pictorial representation of how things relate to each other as a whole, Coggle could be the site for you. Mind maps are useful when you want to ensure that you have an overview and that nothing is left out. They also enable links between areas that can stimulate your thinking and help you to be more critical and analytical.

Padlet

Padlet allows users to upload material (photos, documents or other files) and share this with other Padlet users. For your students, it is a great way of providing a link between the classroom and their home life to encourage learning to go on beyond the institution. Padlet can be used on most devices, such as phones, iPads and tablets, and links multiple users, allowing a sharing of resources and uploaded material. It provides a platform for students to present their material for assessment, such as homework, and for them to contribute to other postings. For embedding, you can upload information sheets and activities, and can comment on the material the students upload to help improve English and maths skills.

Quizlet

Known as the flashcard creator, Quizlet is good for differentiation, revision and embedding literacy, such as through core vocabulary and so on. It can be used on smartphones, tablets, iPads, and most Android devices. Quizlet can illustrate flashcards of items, such as tools and/or materials with key-words/labels underneath. For example, a student can choose a card that you have created with a picture of a torque wrench. The card is clicked on and the name of the item is read out. Clicking again flips it to reveal the picture on the other side.

How to use it: place the definition of a tool or resource in your area on the card and ask the students to match it with the tool/resource. When they flip the card it will reveal the answer. You can do mix and match games where they have to match items to eliminate them and this can be done competitively with others or in an ipsative fashion. There are also existing flashcards that can be searched for and these range from a wide variety of subjects. Students can become familiar with terminology through the use of definitions where they are asked to input into a box what they hear the computer say. This is particularly good, then, for spelling and you can set these up to cover your vocational area (if it is not already available).

Finally, you can generate a new quiz that will test your students' knowledge of terms, tools, or whatever you have included within the area that you have created. There are also several other features and these will become apparent as you become more adept. As with all tools, however, the best way to familiarise yourself is to actually practise using it.

Linoit

This is a sticky-note tool and is good for sharing resources in a user-friendly manner. Both students and tutors can contribute to it. Example: Create a canvas with several sticky notes on the screen and add content to each one. This can be good for revision or for identifying areas where you can embed English and maths. You can also upload documents and insert videos and images. Linoit gets students collaborating and can be good for generating a summary of areas or key points.

Blendspace

Blendspace is used for lesson planning but is also good for flipped learning. It allows web-based materials to connect with other resources and can enable greater embedding when planning. In Blendspace, a range of files can be collated in one area and this forms the basis of the lesson.

You can also search for documents, videos, resources and so on related to your field, depending on the icon you choose. So, if you click on the video icon it will bring up all the videos related to your search term. These can then be selected, dragged and dropped into your lesson. Everything is collated and held within your lesson page. In addition, you can add your own resources or URLs to the existing ones and other users can benefit as you pool resources.

Kahoot

Kahoot is a useful learning platform for stimulating your students, mostly through a quiz. It was devised in Norway in 2013 and has grown into a worldwide tool for learning. The game draws on multiple choice questions and is ideal as a starter activity. However, it can also be used for more substantial classroom activities, as it allows you to incorporate videos and images and can thus link the quiz/game to a variety of teaching resources. Kahoot is fun and user-friendly and is a great way to embed TEL in your teaching. At the time of writing, it was free to use. As with all embedded activities for ICT, Kahoot relies on the smooth and effective running of your classroom technology. You will need strong Wi-Fi and your students will require access to an electronic device such as a tablet, iPad or relevant mobile phone. Here's how it works.

Set the quiz up before the session; a visit to the site will assist you through this process. Your quiz will require multiple answers for your questions and, for differentiation, you may wish to include some answer options that are very similar to the actual answers so that your students have to think carefully. Using your interactive whiteboard or large lecture screen, ask the students to link up via the website. A game PIN (personal identification number) will ensure that only people you want to access the quiz will be able to.

To build on your knowledge of using these tools, the following site, which lists the *Top 200 Tools for Learning*, is useful: **http://c4lpt.co.uk/top100tools/**. Moreover, apps are being created regularly, so it is worth investigating what has been devised since this book was published. As you can see from the address, the site originally listed the top 100 but as time has moved on this has been doubled. Therefore, it is going to be much more beneficial for you to use the internet to keep up to date with what is around. In addition, you can also draw on your colleagues' resources and ideas and online networks that are updated regularly.

In all the activities above, it is worth considering some of the many ways in which you can embed maths and English, as there is much overlap and hopefully the examples will get you thinking.

 Learning exercise

What other social media and use of IT could you use to engage your learners? Whether it is Twitter, Pinterest, Instagram, Snapchat and so on, there will be an app for your learners to engage with that could open up fantastic opportunities for learning. Explore the tools for learning website and make a list of five items that could be useful to you in your teaching.

Virtual learning environments (VLEs)

These are particularly useful in today's education world and many institutions use learning platforms to keep in touch with students. Programs such as Moodle and Blackboard can provide a share point for reaching many students in one hit and can be used to encourage them to engage with technology, as well as posting/uploading files in their own time. As with Facebook and others described above, you can use these to extend the educational potential so that learning is not something that merely happens in your classroom. You can also assess students' work – either formally or informally – through such VLEs and thus monitor their progress. For example, through blog postings you may find that grammar or spelling is a particular bugbear for some students. This can be addressed early on and will help them develop as they prepare to write more academically.

Flipped classroom

In the flipped classroom, students can view a lecture beforehand, via the internet, and use the lesson to debate this. You may also choose to incorporate discovery learning to encourage them to explore a concern without your direct presence, thus developing their autonomy as independent learners. This is more than a 'go off to the library and do some reading' exercise, where it is likely most of them will go home or merely sit and have a chat, even if they actually make it to the library. Of course, students are trustworthy and committed but you will need to keep them motivated.

Technology can be a major player in flipped learning, as your students can use the opportunity to learn independently and an accessible, and mostly straightforward, first port of call is arguably the internet. As such, you can use this to your advantage and signpost them towards an investigation that incorporates innovative uses of TEL without switching them off. Students use technology (as most of us do) daily in their lives and tapping into this massive resource can transform attitudes to learning. For many, TEL is conceptualised more in relation to fun than education which means that the learning can be much more interesting than usual.

By the time you read this, many of the technologies outlined here will have been superseded by more advanced programs and applications. Therefore, these are tasters of how you can incorporate TEL. Some will stand the test of time. Facebook and Twitter, for instance, are still growing in popularity, despite the fact that they are now a number of years old. Where possible, use TEL to embed English and/or maths skills in your lessons to make the most of the learning experience.

Safeguarding and e-safety

A chapter on ICT and TEL would not be complete without mentioning safeguarding. It is worth exploring your institutional policies and consulting an IT specialist to consider the relevant safeguarding procedures and how you can avoid putting yourself in an invidious position. The media have lots of examples of 'unprofessional' conduct in relation to contacting students out of the normal working hours of the college and sharing personal information. It is perhaps surprising for some that a brief internet search can bring up lots of information on a person and this can lead to much unwanted attention. Did you (or do you) have a Facebook account with pictures of you socialising at university? Are these seemingly innocent pictures fuel for the particular technologically savvy student who wishes to discredit you? If you are part of a group forum, what information that is shared is contentious and may need to be acted on from a professional perspective?

 In practice

Kevin, who teaches carpentry, was working with his students in the IT suite as they were design-ing a motif for a fireplace. At the end of the session, his students left but one student had not closed down the computer properly. When Kevin used the task manager to close the program that was causing the issue, he noticed a webpage that had a blog about explosives. He immediately informed the safeguarding officer and the matter was taken to the police. The student was later given support and chose to take on counselling sessions, saying that he had been drawn into the site over several weeks. The official line was that the student was being 'groomed into radical thinking'. Thankfully, a little serendipity and some quick thinking on Kevin's behalf helped steer the student towards a support network that the student was seeking.

These, and many more, considerations – particularly cyberbullying which is a huge field in itself and many books have been written on it – result in your use of technology as being a potential minefield of danger and you will really need to be at the top of your game. On a positive note, you may find yourself in a position to protect a student, as online bullying is now prevalent in lots of areas throughout the world. The main message to take from this is that you will have much research to do in order to capitalise on TEL but this is research that is well worthwhile for your career and your home life. After all, it is difficult these days to avoid technology in most things we do. You will also need to familiarise yourself with your institutional policies on using technology. For instance, do you have a college account for Facebook or WhatsApp? What is the college policy stance on tutors using personal accounts for any apps? This is potentially dangerous terrain and definitely needs exploring.

 Chapter summary

Whether we see students as belonging to a nation that is *digital*, then, or as other writers have argued *Generation Y* (Weiler, 2005) or an *i-Generation* (Rosen, 2010), technology does play a role in many lives and you would do well to utilise it rather than dismiss it. As already argued, TEL can improve learning through greater student engagement, providing fun-related stimulation, and by building on existing interests. Technology is also a core component of much modern employment and, indeed, the way the world is moving. Can you afford to be left behind?

This chapter has covered:

- Digital learners.
- Technology to support employability.
- Technology and fun: whenever the twain meet, the power of teaching is at your feet.
- Tools for learning.
- Virtual learning environments (VLEs).
- Flipped classroom.
- Safeguarding and e-safety.

Further reading

Bavelier, D, Green, CS and Dye, MWG (2010) 'Children, wired: for better and for worse', *Neuron*, 67(5): 692–701.

Passey, D (2013) *Inclusive Technology Enhanced Learning*. London: Routledge.

Whalley, J, Welch, T and Williamson, L (2006) *E-Learning in FE*. London: Continuum.

References

Clark, C and Formby, S (2013) *Young People's Views on Literacy Skills and Employment*. National Literacy Trust.

Helsper, E and Eynon, R (2010) Digital natives: where is the evidence? *British Educational Research Journal*, 36(3): 503–20.

Prensky, M (2001) Digital natives, digital immigrants, *On the Horizon*, 9(5): 1–6.

Prince's Trust (2013) *Digital Literacy Survey*. London: Prince's Trust.

Rosen, LD (2010) *Rewired: Understanding the i-Generation and the Way They Learn*. New York: Palgrave Macmillan.

Weiler, A (2005) Information seeking behaviour in 'Generation Y' students: motivation, critical thinking, and learning theory, *Journal of Academic Librarianship*, 31(1), 46–53.

Useful websites

Animoto – **https://animoto.com/**

Blendspace – **www.tes.com/lessons/xChJhy2BW8Ukhw/what-is-blendspace?redirect-bs=1**

Coggle – **https://coggle.it/**

Digital Unite – **www.digitalunite.com/**

Facebook – **www.facebook.com/facebook**

Kahoot – **https://getkahoot.com/**

Linoit – **https://linoit.com/user/register**

Padlet – **https://padlet.com**

Powtoon – **www.powtoon.com/**

Quizlet – **https://quizlet.com/**

Top 200 Tools for Learning – **http://c4lpt.co.uk/top100tools/**

Twitter – **https://twitter.com/**

WhatsApp – **www.whatsapp.com/**

7

Embedding for inclusion

 ————— This chapter —————

This chapter explores the need to generate inclusive environments in teaching in order to avoid alienating some students. It discusses the importance of incorporating all students and thus catering for a range of diverse backgrounds and experiences, such as those previously marginalised young people who use the FE and skills sector as a second chance for learning. The chapter also explores the thinking that embedding English and maths can support inclusive practices, and how, from a social justice perspective, this can lead to empowerment.

This chapter will cover the following:

- What is inclusion?
- Embedding for inclusion.
- Conceptualising difference.
- Mindset.
- Perceptions of writing.
- Non-conformity or freedom from the pen?
- Capital and literacies.
- Employability.
- Youth offending and social justice.
- Self-esteem and confidence.
- What you can do.

What is inclusion?

In 1996, the Tomlinson report viewed inclusive learning as that which *will improve the quality of learning for students with learning difficulties and/or disabilities* (FEFC, 1996, p13). However, the wider remit of inclusion as reaching out to anyone who may experience exclusion or marginalisation is arguably more relevant, particularly for a sector that *is characterised by many as one of the most inclusive providers of education due to the breadth and depth of the wide range of educational opportunities and qualifications it offers* (Spenceley, 2014, p2).

Learning exercise

Consider the term 'inclusion'. What does it mean to you and your profession? Give an example that you feel illustrates inclusion in your teaching. We will come back to this at the end of the chapter.

Inclusion is about ensuring that all persons belong and can feel a part of the system or community that is created within the institution, and in order to achieve this you may need to make reasonable adjustments to your learning environment (Equality Act 2010). Inclusion is not about segregating young people and educating them in a different setting (this is exclusion) and it is arguably not about preferential treatment (although there may be a balance to redress in some instances). It is about *all* your learners feeling that they are an integral part of the activities, a part of your class, a part of the institution, and so on. It is also not about everyone feeling the same – people are not the same and your learners will benefit most from being treated as individuals – but about everyone feeling that they have the same opportunities and can pursue their goals with no advantage/disadvantage arising from the treatment of others. This is important in FE because many of your students will already be feeling excluded, either socially or educationally or, more likely, both. You are in a fantastic position as an FE teacher in that you can change lives and can salvage those individuals who are heading in a potentially disastrous direction. Thus, the social justice aspect of FE can, and has done for many years, empower young people. Without wishing to sound like a clichéd motivational talk, of course, you really can impact positively on many lives and as most of us come into teaching to make a difference ... why not?

Embedding for inclusion

Education can provide an important contribution to social mobility and is thus regarded as a factor in societal inclusion (Booth and Ainscow, 2011). In many ways, embedding maths and English *is* inclusion. It is about creating opportunities for those who will miss out on social and career mobility because of their labelled ability. This is not their fixed ability, however, merely the level they hold at this time. In her motivationally inspiring Ted Talk in 2014, Carol Dweck (2014) emphasises the power of illustrating to learners that they are *not there yet*, as opposed to suggesting to them that they have failed. (Interestingly, this strategy originally came from a teacher.) The students are still on their journey, then, and have most likely been side-tracked quite significantly because of their experiences.

To conceptualise this in an appropriate manner, think of your role as one of facilitating the next part of their journey. You are not starting with them from scratch just because these are individuals who have previously struggled with maths and English; you are picking up from where they left off and they will have lots of unidentified, or at least unacknowledged, abilities. Be prepared that 'where they left off' may be back in primary school and you could have a lot of work ahead of you. However, in many instances the reason these young people are in this situation is because of missed learning, rather than a lack of ability (although you need to consider the potential support needs for learners with what is currently known as SEND (special educational needs and/or disabilities)). The reasons for their learning gaps may have been due to physical absences or even *cognitive absences*, referring not to a medical condition but to those students who have coasted through many years of their education without anyone truly explaining what they needed or having provided a context for what they were doing. Of course, the blame of educational failure cannot lie solely at the feet of teachers – particularly with so many policy pressures pushing institutions into jumping through performative hoops – but teachers are extremely high in ranking as an educational influence on lives (Hattie 2012). As such, teachers are 'change agents' (van der Heijden *et al.*, 2015) and need to bear this concept in mind as they can empower individuals.

Conceptualising difference

There are many ways of conceptualising individual differences; for instance, various models have been identified to illustrate how reference is made to individuals with learning difficulties and/or disabilities (SEND). The medical/deficit model is in many ways disparaging, as it identifies an individual as a condition. Consider 'an autistic child' as opposed to 'a child with autism', or the term 'hearing-impaired adult', which places the condition first and the individual second. These people are identified by the label and can thus be segregated, even if this is subconsciously enacted. In this way, conditions are often diagnosed in a disease-like manner, with scientists on a quest to 'find a cure' as if there is a risk of contagion. Teachers are generally good at overriding such perceptions, yet it is difficult when an individual is presented in this way. For this child and this adult, it is 'autism' and 'hearing impairment' that defines them.

 Learning exercise

Consider the terms 'black male', 'Asian female' and 'white student'. How do these terms compare to those used in the models of disability? What implications can you identify from using language in varying ways? Are these perceived differently in any way?

In the social model, society is seen to generate many barriers for individuals with disabilities, as it illustrates how social comparisons are made (Oliver, 1990). It is about how society views that particular impairment and considers less the impact on individual lives. In the rights model, individuals are just that – individual – and will be identified in ways such as 'a child with dyslexia', rather than 'a dyslexic child'. This is worth considering in your practice because it discards much of the deficit positioning of the label and can help you to understand some of the barriers many of your students may have faced throughout their lives. And of course, it is not just SEND to which this applies. Do you have learners of varying ethnicity in your class or ethnic students? Whilst recognising differences is important for inclusion, if such differences are foregrounded in too explicit a manner, the difference itself can signify identity, potentially leading us back to stereotypes. In many ways, this is a difficult balance as identities are important and your learners may wish to be known for the strengths of their particular identity.

> The term 'educationally sub-normal' remained in law until 1981.
>
> (FEFC, 1996, p2)

Mindset

In addition to your own awareness raising, your students may also have baggage you may want to check in. That is, negative experiences that shape the way they think which often impinge on their learning. Returning to Carol Dweck's work discussed in Chapter 3, the concept of growth mindset is proving to be an ingredient for success in many schools. It is about tapping into intrinsic motivation but also about improving attitudes so that such motivation becomes more realistic.

Dweck distinguishes between a fixed mindset and a growth one, wherein an individual with a fixed mindset perceives limitations that impact on their self-belief and, subsequently, their performance (perceived as ability). You have probably heard people saying, 'I'm no good at maths', or, 'I can't do English' (pun intended), but this is a self-imposed limitation. Such individuals may have had difficulties with these subjects and this can generate self-doubt. Moreover, it may appear that some people have a disposition for certain subjects, which can also impact on self-belief and constrain actual ability.

 ── Learning exercise ──

Ask your students to say whether they believe that intelligence is fixed at birth or whether it will change as they go throughout life. Note down any evidence they give for their beliefs and how you think this could impact on their learning.

Belief in oneself is nothing new – you may remember the advert for athletes many years back promoting a positive mental attitude – 'PMA' – but the evidence is growing and the implications for education are strong. In particular, the FE sector can benefit from such thinking as low self-esteem and poor confidence are traits of many learners, and these are the ones that have made it to college. Consider the many young people identified as NEET who may never see the opportunities that are available to them. It is arguably important, then, for the FE sector to play a prominent role in social justice – tackling social injustices and empowering its learners. Being NEET is particularly problematic for self-esteem, as around 48 per cent are said to regularly feel low or depressed (Clark and Formby, 2013). While achievements in maths and English do not present a panacea for depression, they can give young people opportunities in life by challenging fixed mindsets.

Perceptions of writing

Recent to the time of writing, the National Literacy Trust released a report based on its sixth annual literacy survey which found that although children and young people's (8–18) reading had 'increased dramatically' and was estimated to continue rising (Clark, 2016, p7), they were writing comparatively less than the previous year. Moreover, the main source of writing appears to be technology-based, such as the various forms of messaging. The report shows that attitudes to writing decline between Key Stage 2 (7–11) and Key Stage 4 (14–16). Crucially, then, FE is an environment where attitudes will have likely declined even further. However, there is hope for salvation in that technology-based writing is still dominant and has the potential to sustain interest for some time. Writing can be fun and entertaining but it has to appeal to the modern world, such as web design or blog writing (see Chapters 5 and 6 for technology-enhanced learning opportunities and strategies for embedding English skills).

 ── Learning exercise ──

Using a typical cohort that you teach regularly, identify those students who you feel are closely representative of Prensky's (2001) concepts of digital natives and/or digital immigrants.

Prior to text messages on mobile phones, writing for students was generally associated with school-books and general academic (or creative) practice. However, there were many outputs, such as the occasional postcard or letter to a friend, a touch of poetry or other creative writing, and even graffiti, which suggested that the act of writing itself was not the problem. It is perhaps ironic to think of someone truanting from an English or art class, only to spend a few hours scrawling their best efforts on the local park wall. Interest in writing, then, may have declined slightly but it will be around for some time and interest in it can be recreated through a little creativity in teaching.

Non-conformity or freedom from the pen?

One appeal of text messages is perhaps the reduced scrutiny of grammar and spelling, and texts are often perceived in a different manner to other forms, particularly handwriting. An open approach to rules in texting is both a strength, in that it can generate interest in writing, and a weakness, as text language can undergo comparatively sudden changes and thus generate confusion. Generally, the grammar and syntax of texting is not challenged and icons and emojis have entered the language, illustrating the use of a combination of words and pictures to represent meaning. Changes are also much quicker than has previously been seen, due to a lack of necessity to be passed by an official board at Oxford. Keeping up with these changes can play a key role in getting your students to engage in reading and writing. Thus, in embedding for inclusion, an understanding of your learners will help you to include them and this in turn will help them to include you – an essential part of the deal as *you* are also becoming a part of *their* lives.

 Learning exercise

Consider the following three questions and then write a brief response for each:

1. How well do you think you fit in with your students?

2. If you were sat in a public place, socialising with a few friends, and a stranger decided to join you, how would you feel: invaded, fine with it?

3. Does knowing a person make it any better if you still struggle to relate to them?

Capital and literacies

In 2008, the National Literacy Trust for Young People found that success in literacy was linked to personal success and happiness, and individuals with poor literacy and numeracy demonstrated a higher probability of being unemployed (Dugdale and Clark, 2008). Building on this, Morrisroe (2014, 5) claimed, *Literacy influences individual capability in all spheres of life. In times of economic instability, low literacy makes individuals and communities more vulnerable to inequality, increasing the risk of social exclusion and undermining social mobility.* Thus, embedding English is a tool for empowerment in many ways. It is your way of facilitating the acquisition of Pierre Bourdieu's concept of cultural capital and of helping your students to develop their literacies (Duckworth, 2014).

Cultural capital, in this sense, refers to the power an individual can have through their knowing in a certain area or their 'legitimate knowledge' (Jenkins, 2006). Such knowledge is thus recognised by those in privileged positions and is given prestige. How well do you know Shakespeare, for instance? And can you use this knowledge to your advantage? As an English literature scholar this could be beneficial, and would position you as having relevant cultural capital in a particular arena, or what Bourdieu (1991) terms 'field', but to what extent is it needed outside of this field? This is a dilemma many of your students will face – such cultural capital is irrelevant for some, so they may experience marginalisation. Your students will probably have social capital (relationships with key figures in the community who are useful to their lives), but this may not be legitimated in elitist circles, such as an educational institution, and cultural capital is often more problematic.

For Bourdieu, this is a necessary means of exchange in certain circles and a lack of it can lead to exclusion. Consider the archaic teaching methods of dealing with a young person who has not yet acquired the established cultural capital: stand in the corner, face the wall, and wear the dunce hat. Whilst we no longer treat individuals in this way, we can alienate them in other ways.

In a similar manner to Bourdieu's capitals, new literacy studies identifies the potential for being educationally and socially literate as one of opening some of the many social- and career-oriented doors. In this way, literacy is not always about English, and students can be computer literate and mathematically literate (numerate). So, embedding English and maths can have a strong social justice slant and this is arguably a key role of FE in today's society.

Employability

Developing skills in English, as we have seen, can impact on employment opportunities. Initially, however, it is about highlighting to your students the need for these skills and the way(s) in which they can be used. In their study for the National Literacy Trust, Clark and Formby (2013, p5) found that *four in 10 children and young people do not appear to see the link between writing skills and their job prospects*. Writing is perhaps deemed to be a literary undertaking for flowery effect: grandiloquence at its best. However, writing is an everyday task and highly necessary to fully function in society. We engage in writing far more than we readily acknowledge and this message is relevant for your students. Developing employability is a significant aspect of inclusion in that it generates opportunities for students to pursue their goals. Much social mobility is based on prestige and this can be acquired in many ways. Moving back to Bourdieu's concept of capitals, cultural, social and economic capital can all play a part.

Youth offending and social justice

Many students entering FE have had problematic experiences of education, particularly if they have been marginalised from a young age, and when combined with poor cultural experiences this can negatively affect their subjectivities (Allan, 2015). Although the landscape of FE is changing, and education is a key factor of everyone's life until the age of 18, there is still a demand for addressing the needs of such young people (Maguire, 2015). Moreover, those previously disengaged at school are said to be more at risk of moving into offending (Farrington, 2007), as they perceive pressure from the apparent need to achieve qualifications in order to secure employment. Many colleges are therefore training staff members in ways of supporting young people who have offended and helping them to refocus on their aspirations. Drawing on the earlier work of Utting (1999), the Youth Justice Board (YJB, 2006, p33) outlined some of the *promising practice indicators* they see colleges using:

- *Collaborative bridging/access programmes with local schools, education authorities, and LSCs to create education and training opportunities.*

- *A student-centred approach, with the emphasis on learning as opposed to assessment.*

- *Curriculum and teaching methods that are sufficiently flexible to take account of individual student needs.*

- *Occupational guidance and work experience that are an integral part of each course.*

- *Effective support for learning such as one-to-one tutoring and pastoral support.*

- *Students following a curriculum that is not only relevant to their current and future needs, but also shows them how they are progressing.*

- *Other support services such as help with transport or childcare.*

- *Joint training for school and college staff on working with young people at risk.*

While all of these are of potential importance for you in your role, the message of individual tailoring of teaching and support is particularly high, and relevance, as seen throughout this book, is a key factor for embedding English and maths.

As an FE teacher, you may work in the prison service, wherein English and maths are particularly important, as skills in these areas are often identified as being far below the national average. This is perhaps a reflection on previous educational disadvantage so even if you are not working in a prison or with learners who have offended, you are still in a position to contribute. Many of those who turn to crime feel that there is no way out and no alternative way of earning a living, and thus exhibit signs of low self-esteem. Education may be conceptualised as only relevant for other people (those with the legitimate capital) and the problem of poor ability in English and maths is perpetuated; as such individuals believe that they were never meant to achieve (Dweck's mindsets?).

Self-esteem and confidence

Low self-esteem can lead to NEET, and Clark and Formby (2013, p9) illustrate how this can be cyclical: *Being NEET also damages young people's confidence, and the longer they are out of work the less likely they are to feel that their confidence will recover.* Without support, and someone to help raise their confidence, some young people can spiral downwards as their ambitions become distant and therefore less and less likely to ever be fulfilled. What can you do, then, to include all your learners and try to avoid this? Help them acquire the skills that will build their confidence, the skills that will enable them to become self-sufficient and thus more autonomous, and the skills for them to understand the dated, but relevant, adage (attributed to Sir Francis Bacon) that knowledge is power. In other words, you are the facilitator to engender literacies and capital to enable them to succeed as autonomous, independent thinkers who have the tools to function in society in a way that is personally beneficial. There are many other aspects of progression and personal development, of course, but our focus here is on inclusion and the potential rewards that ability in maths and English can offer for all individuals.

 Learning exercise

Can you identify two or three students you feel may be suffering from low self-esteem? Revisit their individual learning plans and identify one maths- or English-related strategy that links to one of their personal goals.

What you can do

Inclusion is about identifying those potentially excluded by our practices or, indeed, the system to which we all conform. How inclusive education is, is a contentious area for debate and leads to varying, and often conflicting, viewpoints (Spenceley, 2014). For teachers, however, the focus is on the microcosm, usually the classroom and the extent beyond this where their influence is felt. This means that teachers can employ inclusive practices, even if society (or sometimes the institution) chooses not to. This is not rebellion, of course, and institutions are supposed to be inclusive. However, it is easy to alienate individuals through a focus on conformity, and a default position that the institution is always right can perpetuate the problem. As a teacher, you have the power within your classroom to ensure that an inclusive environment is created and that your students can excel as individuals. Part of this process is arguably the facilitation of maths and English skills as a form of empowerment. In this way, your students will be equipped with the necessary tools, should they choose to compete in society and the job market.

 Learning exercise

Revisit your earlier thoughts on inclusion and its significance for your teaching, and note down any changes in your perception. If nothing is different, consider how abilities in maths and English fit into your initial perception.

 Chapter summary

Inclusion, then, is about involving all your students and ensuring that they feel their contribution is important. While inclusion often focuses on SEND, and aspects such as gender and ethnicity, it is arguably all that and more. We have seen in this chapter that empowerment can arise from the facilitation of maths and English skills and this is arguably a powerful force for inclusion.

This chapter has covered:

- What is inclusion?
- Embedding for inclusion.
- Conceptualising difference.
- Mindset.
- Perceptions of writing.
- Non-conformity or freedom from the pen?
- Capital and literacies.
- Employability.
- Youth offending and social justice.
- Self-esteem and confidence.
- What you can do.

References

Allan, D (2015) Mediated disaffection and reconfigured subjectivities: the impact of a vocational learning environment on the re-engagement of 14–16-year-olds, *International Journal on School Disaffection*, 11(2): 45–65.

Booth, T and Ainscow, M (2011) *Index for Inclusion: Developing Learning and Participation in Schools.* London: Centre for Studies on Inclusive Education.

Bourdieu, P (1991) *Language and Symbolic Power.* Cambridge, Massachusetts: Harvard University Press.

Clark, C (2016) *Children's and Young People's Writing in 2015: Findings from the National Literacy Trust's Annual Literacy Survey.* London: National Literacy Trust.

Clark, C and Formby, S (2013) *Young People's Views on Literacy Skills and Employment.* London: National Literacy Trust.

Duckworth, V (2014) Literacy and transformation, in Duckworth, V and Ade-Ojo, G (eds) *Landscapes of Specific Literacies in Contemporary Society: Exploring a Social Model of Literacy.* London: Routledge, pp27–46.

Dugdale, G and Clark, C (2008) *Literacy Changes Lives: An Advocacy Resource.* London: National Literacy Trust.

Dweck, C (2014) *The Power of Believing That You Can Improve.* Ted Talk. TEDxNorrkoping.

Equality Act 2010. Chapter 15. London: HMSO.

Farrington, DP (2007) Childhood risk factors and risk-focused prevention, in Maguire, M, Morgan, M and Reiner, R (eds) *The Oxford Handbook of Criminology.* Oxford: Oxford University Press, pp602–40.

FEFC (1996) *Principles and Recommendations: A Summary of the Findings of the Learning Difficulties and/ or Disabilities Committee.* Coventry: The Further Education Funding Council.

Hattie, J (2012) *Visible Learning for Teachers.* London: Routledge.

Jenkins, R (2006) *Pierre Bourdieu.* London: Taylor & Francis.

Maguire, S (2015) NEET, unemployed, inactive or unknown – why does it matter?, *Educational Research,* 57(2): 121–32.

Morrisroe, J (2014) *Literacy Changes Lives 2014: A New Perspective on Health, Employment and Crime.* London: National Literacy Trust.

Oliver, M (1990) *The Politics of Disablement.* London: MacMillan.

Prensky, M (2001) Digital natives, digital immigrants, *On the Horizon,* 9(5): 1–6.

Spenceley, L (2014) *Inclusion in Further Education.* London: Critical Publishing.

Utting, D (1999) *A Guide to Promising Approaches.* London: Communities that Care.

van der Heijden, HRMA, Geldens, JJM, Beijaard, D and Popeijus, HL (2015) Characteristics of teachers as change agents, *Teachers and Teaching: Theory and Practice,* 21(6): 681–99.

YJB (2006) *Barriers to Engagement in Education, Training and Employment.* London: Youth Justice Board.

━━ Useful websites ━━

Alliance for Inclusive Education – **www.allfie.org.uk/pages/about/aboutindex.html**

Centre for Studies on Inclusive Education – **www.csie.org.uk/inclusion/legislation.shtml**

Council for the Curriculum, Examinations and Assessment – **http://ccea.org.uk/curriculum/sen_inclusion/inclusion_general_strategies/inclusion**

Department for Education – **www.gov.uk/government/organisations/department-for-education/**

Inclusion Expert – **www.inclusionexpert.com/**

Inclusion International – **http://inclusion-international.org/**

Parents for Inclusion – **www.parentsforinclusion.org/**

United Nations Educational, Scientific and Cultural Organization – **http://unesdoc.unesco.org/**

World of Inclusion – **http://worldofinclusion.com/**

8

Health and social care

Case study

 ── This chapter ──

This chapter presents the first-hand experience of a student who has successfully completed a PGCE in further education and training programme at university. She now teaches health and social care in her local FE college.

Background

Nahleejah was 26 when she returned to learning and a single mum of two young children. At 16, she enrolled on three A level courses at college. However, due to family difficulties, she withdrew in the second year. Her parents split up and Nahleejah lost contact with them, then married and moved away. She obtained work as a porter in a hospital and had aspirations of going to university, although she found parenthood challenging. Nahleejah's husband left her when she was 24 but she eventually settled into a new life, enrolling on a health and social care programme. Despite life pressures, she eventually completed a degree and gained employment in social care. Nahleejah worked in various roles for eight years before she decided she would train to be a teacher. After completing a PGCE in further education and training, she is now working as a teacher in an FE college in the north-west of England. Nahleejah has embraced her personal experiences and acts as a strong role model for her students, particularly anyone from a Muslim background who may feel marginalised or excluded.

Nahleejah's story

I wasn't what you would call a typical Asian student, if there is such a thing. I'm told we are supposed to excel in studying and to achieve high grades, although I guess that's a clear case of generalising, possibly even stereotyping. But I didn't do well at school. I don't believe I was incapable, particularly now as I have achieved a lot since, but I was under pressure to conform and to achieve and stereotypes of high performance didn't help at first. But I turned this on its head and used it to my advantage. I convinced myself that I had it in me to succeed, I just needed some self-belief. I think all the problems at home added up and I broke in the end. I moved into social care because I felt I understood some of the problems of people. And I think I have good empathy, which helps.

My maths and English was all right but it was never strong, especially my maths, and on my teacher training course I needed to have these skills in order to teach others. At first, I thought it would just be about teaching basic stuff for my course area, such as writing letters to clients or applying for jobs, but then it opened up a whole new area of learning for me. I was called on to teach other courses and often stood in for colleagues, and that was daunting at first. One of the English teachers was off and I stepped in for a few weeks. 'You'll be fine with this', my manager said (who was previously my mentor for my teacher training), 'it's just like the embedding activities you did in your PGCE only a bit more depth.' Most of the work was laid out for me but I still needed to know what I was doing. I knew how important maths and English skills were in teaching and in the workplace. We always hear that employers value these skills and if we want to help people secure employment in social care I think it is essential that we give them the tools to do so.

Sarah, health and social care student, year one

Nahleejah's an inspiration, we all love her. She really knows how to motivate us. She told us how she came into FE and I think that's brilliant. It shows us that she's a real person and that she's had a life in the industry and I respect her for that. She knows her stuff but if she gets something wrong she just apologises and we have a bit of a laugh about it. I like that.

The first year was really difficult and on top of all that we were expected to do what they said we needed to complete an English and maths qualification called functional skills. We had sessions on each subject as part of one of our earlier modules and at first I thought this is really weird. *Maths isn't my subject. I don't mind doing a bit of English – I liked that at school – but I think I'm out of my depth with algebra.* I needn't have worried. Despite the fact we never did any algebra anyway, it all made sense. In my area, communication is a central part of providing good care. But it's something we all take for granted. I see it now with some of my students. We interview them for our introductory module and although some of them have a lot of passion for the area (which is essential), they lack communication skills. I try not to turn them away though. I never give up on a student – that's my motto. But our courses are intense so it's only right that we recruit those with the potential to become good carers. We also need students to understand, and embrace, the qualities of diversity and inclusion so that they can tailor their support to an individual's needs. Being in the care industry, the last thing we want is for them to alienate clients.

 In practice

Consider Carol Dweck's research discussed in Chapter 3. Does Nahleejah have a 'fixed' or a 'growth' minsdet? How do you think Nahleejah draws on this to inform her understanding of her own motivation and that of her students? How does her empathy for the students fit into her teaching?

I embed maths and English in my teaching because I have grown to see the importance of these subjects through my work in the college. We have contact with some employers in the area and even though most of our students go to university, that employment link works so well. Our students do work experience known as work-based learning and this gives them an introduction to working in the field. They all say the same, however, in that they really need the maths and English that we help them with. And it has given them so much confidence, which I can empathise with. I was never confident with maths but over the last two years I have learned so much on top of my PGCE. I believe I could actually teach maths as a subject as I enjoy it so much. For me, this is a really weird notion. For a long time, I was that person who said they couldn't do maths. But I overcame my fears and this opened up a new avenue in my career. I no longer worry about not knowing something mathematical and if I do come across something that is unfamiliar I simply Google it or check it out on YouTube. Or failing that, I talk to the A level maths teacher. He's not as grumpy as I first thought and he has some really innovative ways of teaching maths. I find it fascinating, and I never thought I would say that.

On my PGCE course, we had several sessions on embedding English and these opened my eyes to how much we take for granted. We use English skills every day. We write, we text, we e-mail, we post, we blog, we respond to others' comments. And we communicate loads: with our peers, with our families, with our students. Each time we do this we take on a persona that is suitable for the purpose. I have my home life and the way I act there is different to when I have, what I call, my 'teaching head' on. We know this as professionalism but it's more than that. It's what we do and what we do well, so it's something we have to develop rather than learn.

My students are natural communicators – I struggle to shut them up some days – and they seem to be constantly desperate to send that 'really important' text. But if I ask them to write 50 words on the profession, or to stand up and tell the class what they found from their recent job search, they close down. They're not incapable, they just perceive it differently. So I might ask them to start a forum on Moodle or something. Then I post something and try to initiate a discussion. And they post, and they post … and they post! It really opens up the field for communication.

Cade, health and social care student, year one

We did this lesson where we had to research jobs in care and Nahleejah said, 'Get your phone out and Google it.' We looked at her strangely but she said that's what we would do if we were in work and needed to know something. And she's right, we have to remember we're training to work in the care profession. I enjoyed that lesson. I also got to know what Google Scholar was.

One day, five of my students stayed behind as we broke for lunch and as I was packing up my stuff I overheard something. They were still discussing the topic that they had presented to the class earlier. Only, they were far more animated and had some excellent comments that we never saw in their presentation. After apologising for overhearing them, I praised them. I asked if these later thoughts could be put into the forum. I believe that they weren't so much 'later thoughts' though. These were the details that they had held back on in the presentation. Why? I guess they were out of their comfort zone. They were quiet and a bit unresponsive to some questions but they generally covered what I wanted them to. But I'm glad I got to experience this side of them because I grew to see how much they love communicating. My students love to have a voice but I have seen that I need to find the right channel for it to be effective. I'm still working on this but I can see progress.

The biggest thing for me in my teaching was to overcome my fears and I use this to help others. My students have concerns when we mention maths so we tend to skirt round that term. I understand so I feel that it is my job to help them use the strategies that I learned. I struggled with times tables but I don't see this as a major concern. One of my lecturers at university taught me a very easy method of working out the nine times table using my hands. Apparently, they use this in primary schools but I must have missed that day! I switched off from maths at school as I couldn't concentrate. But now I love to help my students. I show them the nine times table on their hands and they love it. It's child-like but very effective. 'And that's one out the way', I say. 'Tomorrow we'll take our shoes off and do the ten times table.' OK, most of them realise that's a joke but it helps with the rapport.

When I first started, some of the students were very challenging. I didn't understand because I thought they chose to come to college. But young people are young people and they need to be motivated, and they needed to feel wanted. I think that is key in teaching. I like all my students, even the ones I don't like, if you catch my meaning. I'm supportive of their needs and I see beyond the façade that often walks into my class on a Monday morning. Some of them are children at heart and they have missed so much. I'm not a replacement for their parents, but I like to model myself as a person they can come to, especially if I'm the only one in their life. I also like to present a good working environment where they can feel safe and want to learn. This is the stuff they talked to us a lot about in university and I can now see its importance. Students have many barriers and they need to know that either they can leave them outside the classroom or we can work together to meet them head-on. I'm not saying I'm a great teacher – I still have lots to learn. But overcoming my own barriers has helped loads.

Commentary

Nahleejah's example of overcoming her personal difficulties is admirable and it has led to her being a more empathetic and understanding teacher. As such, she often knows how to tackle barriers in English and maths. Her positive outlook is a significant message to take from this case study because she has fought against the odds, yet achieved her goals. Nahleejah also collaborates with colleagues in the college and draws on this strategy as a resource. Teaching is often a solitary profession, but it shouldn't be. Sharing perceptions can impact on your own thinking and is often an effective tool for development. It can reinforce your ideas or it can challenge them but, as we have seen throughout this book, challenge is good.

9

Motor vehicle studies

Case study

Jeremy teaches motor vehicle mechanics in college full time. His place of employment is both the college he attended when he left school and where he undertook his PGCE placement. Jeremy was liked so much during his training that a job was created for him.

Jeremy's story

I left school at 16 and enrolled at a local FE college to do motor vehicle studies. My dad was a mechanic so I guess I always thought I would follow in his footsteps. What I didn't realise, though, was how hard it can be and how much maths was needed. I'd seen my dad strip an engine down to the bare bones and if you said to me when I left school that I would have to study maths and English after my GCSEs, I would have laughed. Maths is a very big part of mechanics, though; machinery moves and parts are synchronised with each other. This all requires mathematical timing that you can't just guess. Today's cars in particular are run through computers and if you want to understand how they work you have to get your head around formulae and complex calculations, as well as computer programming. In fact, it was so hard at times that once I mastered it I realised that I had a lot of transferable skills I can utilise in other areas, such as teaching.

Embedding English

I have always struggled with English and for a long time didn't believe that it was for me. 'We're either good at one or the other', my gran used to say. I later discovered that this wasn't so and we could be good at both, but she meant well. And I think evidence has moved on when it comes to learning.

During my PGCE, we looked at ways to incorporate English in our teaching. This frightened me so I enrolled on an evening course to brush up on my spelling. Although I aim to spell correctly, particularly when I'm writing on the board, I realise now it's more important to be honest with your learners. I'm also left-handed so writing on the board is really hard. I tend to rub off what I've written as I go along. But that's another story.

I often apologise and say I've put in two Ss instead of one, or one C instead of two. But I don't make the same mistake twice and once we have had a laugh about it I make sure I won't forget it again. 'We're all learning, all the time', I say to my students. Don't worry if you can't spell a word; just learn it and tomorrow you will be able to spell it. This might sound like a lackadaisical approach to learning English, but believe me it's not. It's about relieving the pressure. This pressure tells us we need to conform, it tells us we are not good at something, and it is a judgement that we don't need. I call it, the Ofsted of ability.

Eddie, motor vehicle mechanics student

My spelling has improved so much and I don't even feel I've been trying. I think the fact that Jeremy doesn't put pressure on us to achieve helps loads. I just learn things as I go along. We do word searches and crosswords and stuff, looking at the terms used in mechanics, and it's all relevant.

For me, restricting ourselves to the belief that we can't do certain things just perpetuates barriers because it heightens the problem which then becomes insurmountable. I was always bad at spelling, but during my PGCE I changed my outlook. I realised that it was more in my head, although I still have to tell myself I can do it at times because my negativity and self-doubt creep in. That's normal, I suppose, and it certainly helps me to understand my students' barriers to learning. Spelling *is* important but the weight behind it is, for me, unnecessary and the pressure becomes bigger than the problem.

In my teaching, I embed both English and maths. For English, I use the GCSE Bitesize website as a guide. My learners who are under 19 need to resit their GCSEs but the ones over 19 can study functional skills. Regardless of what they are working towards, the website has lots of resources and information sheets and it's user-friendly. My English is much better these days but only because I have put the time in. My evening course was tough as I did this at the same time as my PGCE, but I always believe that if you want something out of life you have to work for it.

On the Bitesize website, English language is split into topics and one of these is analysing fiction. For an activity, we discussed the shysters selling written-off cars, known as the 'cut and shut'. This is where two halves of cars have been welded together. It might be that one of the cars was 'rear-ended' while the other one crashed into a lamp post or whatever. One part of each car remains intact and is generally still useable. But mixing the two is dangerous and shouldn't happen. These weren't meant to be together and the way they are welded unprofessionally often results in a weak frame that will definitely endanger lives. If this car is involved in another accident the driver will not have the protection that many cars afford, as well as their insurance being invalid.

The practice of doing this is fraud and as a role play exercise for English and their wider employability skills, my students enact the situation to raise awareness of the dangers. First, they are required to write the advert. Drawing on their persuasive skills and use of similes, metaphors, imagery and connotation, the students engage in some fiction writing. But here is where I think the clever part lies: they write it using the convention of non-fiction for realism but then draw on fictional elements to acknowledge that the whole advert is far from factual.

This draws on two styles of writing at once and is good for getting the students to think outside the box and engage in metacognition as they think about how they learn and the implications for their trade. We then incorporate drama, using role playing to enact the circumstances. One student may play a shyster salesperson whilst another plays a customer. Again, this relies on persuasive argument and the students need to get into the role effectively enough to be convincing. This helps them to empathise with the customer and to point out the danger of abusing mechanical skills. They also have the opportunity to exercise both objectivity and subjectivity.

I also use cloze exercises with the group, mostly as starter activities, which is a strategy I remember from my PGCE. These are good as prompts because you can give them the first letter, or letters within, and then guide them towards what you are looking for. They are particularly good for embedding English as they give prompts and help to stimulate thinking and memory. Also, the students know they need to learn certain terms but they don't see it as spelling or as improving their English. This is effective for those students whose barriers are related to English.

If I mention English to my BTEC group, they often respond by saying things like, 'We're mechanics, not poets.' But this is clearly a misconception. There is far more to English than poetry, although creating a rap to define the coolant system is something I have successfully done with many groups. For me, it's about shutting out what you thought English was, especially if you associate it with school, and then assimilating its component parts (to use the mechanical talk) and re-assembling it for meaningful content.

For spelling, we have tried the 'look, cover, write, check' method that my wife showed me. She works in a primary school and my initial reaction was dismissive as my students are not children. But adults respond well to a bit of fun and this exercise is not childish at all. It is actually very effective, as it draws on the visual aspect. I have found that spelling is visual and seeing the word really helps students to lay it down in their memories. Another method for improving spelling is the use of anagrams, and this is even more effective. A student may misspell a word but because they have all the letters for that word, they will be aware that there are more, or fewer, letters in the word than they have used. They then persist with the activity until they solve it. For added interest, I combine this with a word search, so the learners need to unscramble the words and spell them correctly before they attempt to find them. For my more advanced learners, I might only include words in the word search that are synonyms of the ones they have rearranged from the anagrams, rather than the actual words. The level of learning deepens as a result and the exercise becomes more meaningful and more difficult to do, so everyone's happy.

Embedding maths

Because I was fairly good at maths, I don't really have any difficulty in embedding it within my teaching of mechanics. The hardest part is thinking of something a little more creative because I don't like to run through mundane stuff just because we need to cover it. I find that my learners learn more efficiently and effectively when the lesson is interesting. This also prevents my teaching from becoming stagnant, which I see in my colleagues. Most of the staff here are enthusiastic, use variety in their teaching, and take their CPD seriously. One or two others, however, refuse to develop. Some of them have been teaching the same subject for 30 years and their teaching has changed little. They even complain if the subject content changes. But that's progress. We don't drive the same cars as we did 30 years ago. I came to this college to do mechanics and some of those teachers taught me. But now they're looking at early retirement because they struggle at embedding English and maths. I find this narrow-mindedness to be tragic.

Shirley, motor vehicle mechanics student

I'm not very good at maths but I am good at English so I've made loads of suggestions to Jeremy for what we could do. He's great, he always listens to me and most of my ideas have been used in our lessons where I help some of the others. I think being the only girl on the course has been an advantage. The boys listen to me and they appreciate my help. I'll probably end up being a teacher one day.

We are all learning, all of the time. I learn loads from my students because I'm open to listening. And I use my knowledge of my colleagues to keep my teaching fresh, which pays off because I can be creative with English and maths. The moral, then, if there is one, is: stay positive and be motivated by negative experiences as well as positive ones.

In a typical mechanics session, we might look at calculating torque or the rotation of an axis. However, I also do more functional-type questions with the students that look at real-life contexts. For instance, we would do simple stuff like looking at the prices and types of engine oil and deciding on which one was best. And then we would provide estimates for services, including pricing brake pads, oil filters and so on, and a costing for labour on top, as well as sometimes including reductions for percentages or fractions. This helps the students identify a profit margin. Some of the calculations are straightforward so we also investigate work, energy and power, which results in some complex calculations using formulae. Other examples include the study of kinematics to understand movement and acceleration. For progression, this gives the students a taster for considering university-level study, as well as thinking about moving into the profession itself.

Commentary

Jeremy's narrative focuses more on English than maths and this is testament to the work he has put in, as this was originally his weaker subject. Jeremy is passionate about what he does and this clearly shows as those around him, such as his students and his colleagues, both admire and respect him. Whilst it is rare to have a job created for you, it does illustrate how professionalism and enthusiasm can pay off. As well as his teaching role, Jeremy mentors students undertaking a PGCE.

Having undertaken his own journey of development in English, he is representative of the benefit of stretch and challenge and I am confident that he will continue learning throughout his career. His students report that his lessons are fun, interesting and thoroughly engaging, and that the maths and English they do are relevant.

10
Hair and beauty
Case study

 —— This chapter ——

Adelajda completed a PGCE and qualified as a teacher four years prior to the time of writing and this case study was originally going to be about her. However, she suggested that it would be more useful to have the voice of one of her students. Therefore, this case study focuses on the perspective of Jessica, a hair and beauty student working towards an NVQ level 2, and resitting her maths GCSE, in a further education college in the north of England.

Jessica says that she knew from an early age she wanted to gain skills in hair and beauty but was unsure of whether this would lead to a career or a hobby. She claims that she hated her maths resit at first but that it got easier as she eventually saw opportunities where she could apply some of the maths in her training.

Jessica's story

When I came to college, I had to resit maths but because I got a B in English they were happy with that. I didn't really know what I wanted to do as a job, but I knew I wanted to develop my knowledge in hair and beauty. I thought that I would end up doing something else – I don't know what – and that hair and beauty was just a hobby. But I didn't have a clear goal in mind so I started with the hair and beauty to see where that would lead me. Once I got going with it I loved it and knew then that it is something I will do until I am much older. I may have a change of career when I get in my 40s – I saw my mum go through that – but I think the hair and beauty industry will be with me for life, as I can always do it for friends.

The course was great and we were expected to do maths and English all the way through but it never felt as if we were doing it. I knew we were because they had told me when I started, but I forgot about that side of it until a few months into the course. Adelajda said to me, 'We need to get you through all the criteria for maths and English. I know you will have your GCSEs but you need to know how to use these skills.'

'OK', I replied, thinking that there was going to be extra maths and English sessions and then one day she said, 'Right! This is what we are going to cover in the next few weeks.' I nodded as usual and then panicked when I saw all these terms: ratio and proportion, percentages, reading data, and so on. 'Do I have to do all that on top of my course?' Adelajda smiled and then reminded me what we had already covered. And I couldn't help but smile back when she explained to me what they were.

The maths and English was very much tied in with the course and it made us see just how important these skills are if you are serious about your career. In the ratio sessions, we mixed hair products and looked at the legal requirements for working with chemicals. I began to see that styling someone's hair was more complicated than I first thought. I also thought that everything would be practical and that I would hate any academic work, such as writing up what we had done. But I didn't! I loved every minute.

When colouring hair, a mistake in the correct proportion of developer to colour can look awful. But I never saw this as maths. I thought of it as just something you need to learn. The tutors tended to refer to the maths skills as hair and beauty skills – which they are – and then later on they would explain what we had done. For example, Adelajda spoke of getting the right ratio of product in to achieve the right mix and she showed us how the colours appeared on the spectrum. What she wasn't doing was saying, 'You need to do mathematical ratio this week to cover the maths skills.' But I guess we would have switched off if she had said it that way. Everything was related and everything made sense.

> **Adelajda**
>
> *I try not to put too much emphasis on embedding because it can be seen as another chore for the students. I like to draw their attention to the English and maths we've covered but I don't make too much of it at the time. It's just what works for me. When I start with, 'We need to embed these maths skills etc.' you can hear the groans echo across the college.*

One time, we were asked to devise a business model over the coming lessons. I think we had about six weeks to do it and we were told that we would have to research the market. There was lots of maths involved with the estimating of profit and loss for our accounts, and great use of English as we drafted up a letter to the bank saying why we needed a business account and overdraft. For clients, we wrote to several businesses in the area and suggested that we could provide a lunchtime hair styling service known as the 'half-hour hair dos'. I thought this was a great idea, as it really capitalised on our time and meant that if we had to take anyone on we knew for certain what time period we would need to pay them for.

So we designed a survey for the businesses and we used the data that we felt we would have retrieved (had we really been in a position to send this out) to estimate the potential business we would have, to calculate the costs for products and staffing, and to work out the time involved overall. I was in charge of drafting up a letter and I was allowed to research this using the internet. I found a template from a website called Dummies (**www.dummies.com/**) and used this as my guide. I then wrote under the headings and found that this was much easier to do than sitting with a blank piece of paper and thinking, what should I say? How should I start it? Even though it seems like a sole task, I relied on the team to provide information for the letter, so we worked collaboratively.

Adelajda informed us that teamwork is an important element of running a business and that the whole team was only strong when all the cogs in the system worked together. I enjoyed this process and I believe that it is important because working within hair and beauty is about your social skills as well as English and maths. Working with clients, we are required to be sociable and to be quite thick-skinned against the awkward ones. I was quite surprised to learn that these skills were part of an English syllabus. I remember doing speaking and listening at school and we did some drama exercises, but I never connected the dots to teamwork.

So, we did mock job interviews and role-playing scenarios with clients (some more difficult than others) to fully experience the life of a hair and beauty specialist. Luckily, I'm quite a chatty person and I like meeting new people, so this wasn't a problem. But some of the others would struggle, so I can see why it was important to practise these skills. We later put these to use properly when we worked with actual clients. At first, we would just say hello and chat about the weather or whatever but then we got to get to know them better and it got easier. I also saw that this is part of our service, as it's sort of expected. So even though we were covering speaking and listening it was all good fun. And clients tend to go with someone they know. It's all about trust.

—— In practice ——

In experiential learning, students are encouraged to immerse themselves in an activity that enables a more concrete form of learning. It is the experience itself which adds meaning to the learning. In plumbing, for instance, pipework is experiential. The act of bending the pipes, attaching extensions, and cutting the required length requires the student to engage with the activity (experience) rather than watching a video or hearing about it in a lecture.

In relation to other English skills, we had to design a flyer to promote the business. I began to realise that quite a lot goes into a flyer and in the very best ones it's *every* word that makes a difference. We drew on persuasive language, needing to be really descriptive with rich language that makes someone want to come to you for their business, and stylistic tricks of the trade such as catchy sentences and key phrases such as, 'only £19.99' rather than £20, and 'professional service in a relaxing and caring environment'. Also, these needed to be proofread for professionalism and the narrative needed to give us an edge over our competitors. I applied short, sharp sentences to create a punchy feel in the text and used bullet points for the busy modern reader. We also looked at flyers for other businesses and critiqued them. Some were really amateurish and I wondered why they bothered wasting their money in that way.

I also incorporated maths and got to use the mean, median, mode and range that I already knew about. I was amazed because I thought it was useless stuff that I'd never need in life, but when we did our project and had to work out how much we thought we would earn so we could average it out I thought it was really good. The prices varied a lot but we could estimate what we thought would give us a good return and that helped us to work within a budget. So, although I was never keen on maths, I began to see that it is so important for the trade and I cannot imagine how anyone can get along with only a surface knowledge of it.

An important part of the design of our flyers was the professional look and we had several ICT lessons to achieve this. What I didn't realise at the time was that we were even doing maths when we designed it. We looked at the measurement for a typical flyer and in the guidelines the details were in inches, so we had to convert it to millimetres and centimetres. I've never been good with stuff like this but Adelajda showed me that I could use a ruler to help me to visualise it. I had no idea what 15cm looked like but seeing it on the ruler helped me to gauge other measurements. We did an activity where we were asked to guesstimate the size of a paperback novel and mine was the closest. I think it was easy. I just visualised it in relation to the ruler and imagined holding it. I also do this for other measurements. For instance, we needed to apply 300ml of liquid to a mixture and the first thing I thought of was a Coke can.

In one of our lessons, we looked at a variety of everyday objects – shopping items and so on – and guessed their weight or how much liquid they held. These included the number of grams in a tin of beans or a bag of sugar, the weight of an average pizza, and how much orange juice was in a large carton. I enjoyed this lesson as it seemed like we were having a break from our hair and beauty training. And I even got to find out what a centilitre was, which I honestly had not heard of until that moment. This was all relevant, though. We were estimating weights and liquids and building our maths skills for our subject. So I guess there were times when I was doing hair and beauty and I didn't realise we were doing maths, and there were times when we were having a bit of fun with 'life stuff', as I like to call it, and we were also doing maths. It seems to have been designed very cleverly and I wouldn't have it any other way. They knew what they doing in the college – I can see that now – and all they were doing was dressing it up in a fun way as they showed us the relevance of English and maths.

Commentary

Jessica's reconceptualisation of maths was an extremely significant turning point in her life as she now has an ambition to do a science degree later in life. Although this is unrelated, she feels that it has opened up new horizons for her career path.

> *I'll still do the hairdressing because it's in my blood. But Iḋ love to travel and learn about science. I love learning about the environment and I don't think this is beyond my reach any more. I never thought Iḋ say this but maths is actually quite fun. Who knows where it will lead?*

11

Construction
Case study

 ── This chapter ──

Robbie, an ex-construction apprentice, works as a lecturer in a community college. In his teaching, he embeds English and maths with great enthusiasm and aims to motivate students through his passion for personal development.

Robbie's story

I struggled with the environment of my school because I grew up in what some people would call a 'hard' area. We saw the teachers as idiots and it was very much a 'them and us' attitude. I used to think, it's OK for you, you've had a privileged upbringing, you're getting paid well, whereas we don't know what the future holds for us. But, I realised that we can have a say on our future.

I was temporarily excluded from school and they put me on a work-based learning programme. They asked me what I wanted to do and said I could choose. They said we would have 'a carousel of activities'. I didn't know what that meant at the time but I got to try out different vocations, so I didn't care. Surprisingly, construction is the one I excelled at and once they agreed that I could do that for three days a week, I made it my ambition. I didn't know anyone who was a builder so I can't really say where the urge came from. I just liked it; I felt it was the real me. By the time I finished my GCSEs, I had secured a place with a construction firm. They had been in to see us in our placement and said I made an impression on them so I applied. Fortunately, my maths and English was always strong. I remember my reports saying, 'Robbie is clever but fails to apply himself.' Well, I've certainly applied myself now.

As I worked through my construction apprentice, it reaffirmed my belief that English and maths are important in everyday life and strong skills in these areas will boost career opportunities. I am currently in the first year of my role as lecturer in a community college and I teach the Level One Certificate in Construction Skills. My students are required to draw on the skills of English and maths to support their knowledge and I achieve this through a variety of means. To me, construction is not only a significant industry to work in, it is as important as the medical profession. Lives depend on the foundations and generally secure nature of our buildings and I believe that academic learning should also underpin the practical application of the business. While it is arguably not as respected as the medical profession, it is up to us as agents to raise the awareness of how significant it is. Many students are steered towards practical learning activities at school because it is believed that they are incapable of performing well in academic subjects such as science, maths and English. However, if we raise the status of areas such as construction, this would challenge such thinking.

Oliver, construction and the built environment student

Robbie is a wealth of knowledge, you can ask him anything. He's been there and done it but he's not arrogant which makes him a great teacher. He's so interested in everything he does, he inspires us. Sometimes he just stops what he's doing and tells you a really interesting story about when he worked in the building trade. I love those moments.

Examples of how I embed maths and English skills

In one activity (over four weeks), I asked the group to provide the college with a quote for building an extension on the current gymnasium. The activity involved numerous tasks which we broke up as follows.

Maths

Measure, shape and space/Basic number calculations

First, the area needed measuring, so one person visited the site to provide a free estimate. This involved measuring skills and general construction awareness (e.g. where are the drains, are these affected, can they be moved? How solid is the earth and how deep are the footings likely to be?). Once this information was known, calculations were made for two employees (labour) to dig out the area. Calculations included the following:

- the daily rate;
- how many days it would take based on the width and depth of the footings and whether half-days would be considered;
- what machinery (if any) would be needed and costs (daily rate, weekly rate and so on);
- other materials.

Number operations/Area and perimeter

The size and format had to be established in conjunction with the client's (my role in the activity) wishes, so these were provided. Other calculations were also needed for the building itself. The students calculated the cost of materials by researching prices online (*collecting and interpreting data*). These included the type of roof and number of doors and windows, as well as more obvious features such as the number of bricks. The flooring area was calculated in metres squared for floor tiles and the perimeter was measured in metres for skirting. Packs of floor tiles were priced once it was established how many would be needed. The roof was calculated in a similar way, taking into account its shape and structure. For instance, is it a flat roof? Does the roof have an apex and sides?

Labour costs for the main project were calculated and added on to the labour costs above, taking into account the mixture of skilled and unskilled employees for the varied costs. What professions are needed? Plumbers, builders, carpenters and so on.

The students also calculated a cost for *planning permission* for the extension to be built and *advice and guidance*, wherein a team would provide support throughout the process.

English

Format/style/grammar/punctuation

The following questions were considered:

- How is the quote presented?
- Is it written formally and professionally?
- Are headings/sub-headings/bullet points used?
- Is the format reader-friendly?

- Is the text overpowering and difficult to read, with no paragraphs or spacing?

- Has it been proofread?

- Is the accompanying narrative inviting?

Language is crucial in the construction trade, particularly for sales when providing a description of what the client can expect. For this, we discussed differences such as, 'a luxurious, Edwardian-style exterior with a contemporary, open-plan inside' and 'a rectangular building with a sloping roof.'

Speaking and listening

- How is the project communicated in other ways? Face to face or telephone?

- Does the construction adviser present him/herself well?

- Do they promote trust and professionalism?

- Are they convincing in their demeanour?

To illustrate another example from my course, I asked the group to provide a quote for a bridge and to liaise with the relevant organisations to encourage them to sanction the bridge and to see that its implementation was conducted within the necessary legality. In many ways, the above points for maths and English were applicable to this project too. However, there were other factors that we drew on from maths and English in a way that was unique to the type of quote. For instance, the weight of the bridge was needed and this informed the type of materials that could be used. It also required specialist provision in the form of a structural engineer and this can often be an additional cost if it requires an external or freelancer engineer, depending on the construction company.

> ### Henry, construction and the built environment student
>
> *We do lots of really good projects and they go on for weeks. It's hard because you can't have a day off in case you fall behind. But I try not to have days off anyway because you miss out on too much and I really enjoy it. You think English is boring but we have a laugh doing role plays and I like writing letters to clients because I wasn't good at it in school and I want to run my own business in a few years.*

As the bridge would be arched, the estimation of materials for the floor would need to take this calculation into account. Therefore, a straight path between the two points would provide an inaccurate measurement and the arch would depend on the gradient, which would also need to factor in the load – a perhaps complex calculation for the non-specialist. As a team, we also asked ourselves whether or not there were any organisations that the company would need to communicate with in order to acquire the necessary permissions and to undertake the calculations, such as legal requirements on the materials, the span, the weight, the gradient and so on, and general building regulations.

We drew up a letter to the local authority in the first instance to outline our plans and to obtain permission. This had to be professional in its format, and it needed to be clear and thus illustrate a strong degree of literacy. We structured the letter in a way that would employ persuasive language in order to argue the necessity for the bridge and to illustrate our experience and ability to see the project through to completion. We then drafted an e-mail to the structural engineer to see if we could acquire a quote. Although the tone of the e-mail was mostly formal, the format was different from the letter. We were able to include hyperlinks in the e-mail to a basic web page that we designed in WordPress. This page displayed information on the team and hypothetical company, with an example of how the end product was envisaged. Such use of technology is crucial in today's world and can really boost the communication between a company and a client and allows for vast amounts of information to be accessed quickly. Moreover, using this medium we were also in a position to promote Facebook, Twitter and LinkedIn accounts to generate further advertising.

 In practice

Metacognition is commonly known as thinking about thinking and it has been shown to have an average impact on learning of around eight months (Higgins *et al.*, 2012). When a student considers the process of learning – how they got to that particular resolution, what worked, what didn't – they engage in metacognition. This can help them to understand themselves more and identify the strategies that work for them. Questioning your students and encouraging them to reflect and become more self-aware can stimulate metacognition.

After acquiring building regulations approval, the next step was to design how we would erect the bridge in a safe and effective manner, conforming to the Building Act 1984 and the Construction (Design and Management) Regulations 2015. This would also ensure that the bridge was safe to use and could carry the load that we had calculated. These policy documents need to be interpreted in a way that closely aligns with the policymakers' intentions and this often requires a high level of comprehension. As such, English is a crucial aspect of the project.

In summary, calculations were undertaken for the bridge requirements (geometry, formulae and so on), letters and other types of communication were used (writing, speaking and listening, persuasive language and so on), and policy documents needed to be understood and implemented (reading comprehension, handling data and so on). These are just some of the areas covered in this project and many more can be identified.

Commentary

This case study illustrates the use of maths and English skills in the construction industry and it is interesting that Robbie touches on the (arguably class-based) lack of parity of esteem between academic and vocational learning. His example of the medical profession is strong and this can be seen further through the application of learning. Some medical practitioners advance in their careers as a result of their practical ability. For instance, a surgeon operating on patients is required to demonstrate their skill in using tools and manipulating instruments to perform corrective surgery, while a general practitioner (GP) is perhaps paid for a level of knowledge in illness and disease and the medical treatment of these. In many ways this is a simplistic observation – the surgeon will obviously engage conceptually while GP work involves much hands-on activity. However, there is an argument to suggest that while many practical aspects of the medical profession are valued (and rightly so), general perceptions of construction do not appear to equally value the vocational element. The focus here is on the conceptualisation of the learning that is occurring, of course, not each profession's value in relation to humanity, as this is perhaps a persuasive factor.

References

Higgins, S, Kokotsaki, D and Coe, R (2012) *The Teaching and Learning Toolkit*. London: Education Endowment Foundation.

Useful websites

Building Act 1984 – **www.legislation.gov.uk/**

Construction (Design and Management) Regulations 2015 – **www.legislation.gov.uk/**

Appendix

Embedding English and maths: an institutional approach

In response to the growing number of students in FE, Ofsted (2015) offer four case studies of how colleges are successfully implementing the study of English and maths. This document is available online and there is a link below. It is worth exploring as it illustrates real examples of successful practice in the sector.

As well as teachers, it is arguably useful for managers and leaders as it can help them to understand the implications for teaching. Examples include:

- expectations on all vocational teachers to embed GCSE English and maths in their teaching;

- adopting a whole-school approach;

- remuneration for currently outstanding teachers to extend their teaching ability to accommodate English and maths or a vocational area;

- building links with families (for support) and employers (for relevance).

In the document, this rather inspiring quote from a teacher illustrates the potential for such changes to be implemented: *We've come out of our comfort zone by having to learn how to teach GCSE, so we now need to help our students come out of theirs* (Ofsted, 2015, p3).

Reference

Ofsted (2015) *Increasing Provision in English and Mathematics through Strategic Planning*. Available at: **www.gov.uk/government/uploads/system/uploads/attachment_data/file/470267/English_and_maths_in_FE_colleges_-_good_practice_example.pdf**.

Appendix

Embedding English and maths: an instructional approach

Index